Because we never said goodbye

More poems from Charlbury

Because we never said goodbye

*More poems
from Charlbury*

*Compiled by
Rob Stepney*

THE WYCHWOOD PRESS

Our books may be ordered from bookshops or (post free) from
Evenlode Books, Market Street, Charlbury, OX7 3PH
01608 819117

E-mail: wychwood@joncarpenter.co.uk

Credit card orders should be phoned or faxed to 01689 870437 or 01608 811969

A share of the proceeds from each copy sold will go to the Charlbury Cricket Club Pavilion appeal

First published in 2008 by
The Wychwood Press
an imprint of Jon Carpenter Publishing
Alder House, Market Street, Charlbury, Oxfordshire OX7 3PH

The poems are the copyright of the contributors

All illustrations including the cover picture are copyright Mick Rooney RA

The right of the named contributors and artist to be identified as authors of the works attributed to them has been asserted in accordance with the Copyright, Designs and Patents Act 1988

All rights reserved. No part of this publication may be reproduced, stored in a retrieval system or transmitted in any form or by any means electronic, mechanical, photocopying or otherwise without the prior permission in writing of the publisher

ISBN 978-1-902279-34-3

Manufactured in England by Cpod Ltd., Trowbridge BA14 0XB

Introduction

For the first volume, people fished poems out of drawers. For this one, many contributors have written especially for the book. Some even rose to the challenge of finding a rhyme for "Charlbury". There is a wonderful appetite in the town for writing poetry, and for hearing it read.

When arranging these poems, some seemed to flow naturally one into another, while others are so contrasting that they provoke you to place them together. Marvellously, people want to say a huge number of different things but all in a way that is somehow more powerful or entertaining than everyday prose. To encompass the great diversity, we've had to introduce a colour supplement with sections on gardening, art, cookery, travel and motoring – if that's not too grand a term for what one does in a Reliant Robin.

Sales of the first volume, together with the evening of readings in the Memorial Hall, raised £670 for the Shorthampton Church maintenance fund. Soon after the 2007 flood damage, Jon Carpenter (of Evenlode Books) and I decided that the Charlbury Cricket Club appeal should be a beneficiary of this new compilation. Our sincere thanks to all who have contributed.

I have been grateful for the advice of Hilda Reed and Ed Fenton when compiling this book. And it is a great privilege to have had Mick Rooney RA paint its cover and provide illustrations for the inside.

Rob Stepney
Walcot, September 2008

Contents

I Love and loss   p15

A massage for my mother	Brigid Avison
The everyday moment	Anthony Landale
Remind me to breathe	Mark Moss
As if translated from the Persian	Mick Rooney
Peace of mind	Tim Crisp
Blue baby I and II	Hilda Reed
A fine romance	Malcolm Gibb
High-rise loving	Bella Hewes
Chariots of desire	Mick Rooney
A paraphrase of "Vides ut alta"	Elizabeth Llewellyn-Smith
Lionel	Philip Drew
Encounter	Jane Corbett
Tandem nursing	Kat Patrick
Love's the meaning of life	Peter Head
Feeding the wolf	Anthony Landale
Epitaph I and II	Mick Rooney
A good soldier	John Lanyon
Footsteps	Moira Wyatt
Requiem	Robert Macefield
Our loss	Peter Head
Sunset hours	Rosa Young
Last respects	Eileen Dore
Charlie's demise	Eileen Dore
True voice	Anthony Landale
Sleep love	Moira Wyatt
Love	Dee Moss
Colouring in literature	John Lanyon
Does nothing rhyme with Anthony?	Kate Smith
Labour report	John Lanyon
A Dad in a million	Tim Widdows
Mums of the world	Tim Widdows
Inheritance	Marjorie Mayhew
Decisions	Marjorie Mayhew
Three more weeks to go	Rebecca Collins

II River and stone   p45

A walk in winter   Hilda Reed
Dreams of Mother Evenlode   Mark Moss
Beating the bounds   Ian Colville
Does nothing rhyme with Charlbury?
   Something does   Angus Bentall
   Rhyme   Dorothy Day
   Limerick   Leah Fowler
   What rhymes with Charlbury? Dee Moss
These feet   Mark Moss
Dry stone walls   Igor Goldkind
England   Patricia Perry
O Charlbury fish van   Adrian Lancini
Rain, rain, go away   Peter Barber
The great flood   Rebecca Collins
Oxfordshire 2007   Keith Fountain
In Finstock Field   Gareth Miller
He dwells in the ground of my being Jenifer Brown
Port Meadow   Gareth Miller
Charlbury's full of ceorls   Mark Moss
In Charlbury town   Hilda Joy Jones
The people we know   Rebecca Collins
Charlbury's contrasting worlds   Bella Hewes

III Shorts   p69

Walcot illuminations   Sarah Geeson Brown
The hardships of North Berwick, and other short poems
                        Arthur Crisp
Bulb   Mick Rooney
Browing old gracefully, and other bits and bobs
                        Rob Stepney

IV Pastimes: the Colour Supplement   p75

A circle of friends   Philip Drew
About Blue   Rob Stepney
Homecoming   Eileen Dore
Young Tolly   Elizabeth Llewellyn-Smith
The choir   Sheila Peacock

Suppertime blues	John Lanyon
Help!	Margery Mayhew
Keep fit	Gareth Miller
The undressed chef	Nick Owen
Hedgehog en croûte	Nick Owen
Tiramisu	Bob Cockburn
The Lowry collection	Michael Moss
The portrait	Moira Wyatt
The straight lines of Giza	Mark Moss
DIY islands: Madeira	Peter Barber
Skiathos	Elizabeth Llewellyn-Smith
Bad things were done in Ephesus	Rob Stepney
Follow my lieder	Mick Rooney
Swagbelly	John Lanyon
Farewell Fiesta	Tim Widdows
Night life	Dorothy Day
The countryside	Dorothy Day

V Past times   p95

Shards of now	Mark Moss
Winter bath	Hilda Reed
You nudged my muse	Eithne Dillon
We who remain	Robert Macefield
A dream of our youth	Peter John Colyer
Then	Brigid Allen
Memories of Witney	Eileen Dore
Thoughts	Eileen Dore
Summer '95	Eileen Dore
Cobwebs	Gareth Miller
Christmas spirit	Moira Wyatt
Echoes of summer in Pazenas	Moira Wyatt
Cricket at Worcester	Mike Dix
Damp wait	Mike Dix
The school walk	Moira Wyatt
Cissie Gomm	Ethel Thornett

VI A rich miscellany   p111

Is there a book inside you?	Adrian Lancini
An ABC of poetry	Rob Stepney

Words	Eithne Dillon
Mercy	Anthony Landale
Dreamwalker	Robert Macefield
Transience	Jane Corbett
Always whispering	Anthony Landale
Jam and Jerusalem	Tim Widdows
Braggadocio	John Lanyon
World like mine	Peter Head
The case for late October	Mick Rooney
October Evensong	Gareth Miller
Dear Nine-to-Five Existence	Adrian Lancini
Sisters	Hilda Reed
Vic's sticks	Eithne Dillon
Sculpture of life	Peter Head
Seed	Robert Macefield
Mystery	Robert Macefield
Head bus driver	Anon
When might time have stopped?	Rob Stepney
Nocturne	Gareth Miller

Poets in alphabetical order

Anon	Head bus driver	129
Brigid Allen	Then	103
Brigid Avison	A massage for my mother	15
Peter Barber	Rain, rain, go away	60
	DIY islands: Madeira	88
Angus Bentall	Something rhymes with Charlbury	50
Jenifer Brown	He dwells in the ground of my being	63
Bob Cockburn	Tiramisu	84
Rebecca Collins	Three more weeks to go	43
	The great flood	61
	The people we know	66
Ian Colville	Beating the bounds	49
Peter John Colyer	A dream of our youth	102
Jane Corbett	Encounter	24
	Transience	117

Arthur Crisp	The hardships of North Berwick and other poems	71
Tim Crisp	Peace of mind	18
Dorothy Day	Rhyme	50
	Night life	93
	The countryside	94
Eithne Dillon	You nudged my muse	99
	Words	115
	Vic's sticks	124
Mike Dix	Cricket at Worcester	107
	Damp wait	108
Eileen Dore	Last respects	33
	Charlie's demise	33
	Homecoming	78
	Memories of Witney	103
	Thoughts	104
	Summer '95	105
Philip Drew	Lionel	23
	A circle of friends	77
Keith Fountain	Oxfordshire 2007	62
Leah Fowler	Limerick	51
Sarah Geeson Brown	Walcot illuminations	71
Malcolm Gibb	A fine romance	20
Igor Goldkind	Dry stone walls	54
Peter Head	Love's the meaning of life	25
	Our loss	31
	World like mine	120
	Sculpture of life	126
Bella Hewes	High-rise loving	20
	Charlbury's contrasting worlds	67
Hilda Joy Jones	In Charlbury town	66
Adrian Lancini	O Charlbury fish van	58
	Is there a book inside you?	113
	Dear Nine-to-Five Existence	122
Anthony Landale	The everyday moment	16
	Feeding the wolf	27
	True voice	34
	Mercy	116
	Always whispering	117
John Lanyon	A good soldier	28

	Colouring in literature	36
	Labour report	38
	Suppertime blues	81
	Swagbelly	92
	Braggadocio	119
Elizabeth Llewellyn-Smith	A paraphrase of "Vides ut alta"	22
	Young Tolly	79
	Skiathos	88
Robert Macefield	Requiem	30
	We who remain	101
	Dreamwalker	116
	Seed	127
	Mystery	128
Margery Mayhew	Inheritance	41
	Decisions	42
	Help!	82
Gareth Miller	In Finstock Field	62
	Port Meadow	64
	Keep fit	82
	Cobwebs	105
	October Evensong	121
	Nocturne	132
Dee Moss	Love	35
	What rhymes with Charlbury?	51
Mark Moss	Remind me to breathe	16
	Dreams of Mother Evenlode	47
	These feet	52
	Charlbury's full of ceorls	65
	The straight lines of Giza	87
	Shards of now	97
Michael Moss	The Lowry collection	86
Nick Owen	The undressed chef	83
	Hedgehog en croûte	83
Kat Patrick	Tandem nursing	25
Sheila Peacock	The choir	80
Patricia Perry	England	56
Hilda Reed	Blue baby I and II	19
	A walk in winter	47
	Winter bath	98
	Sisters	123

Mick Rooney	As if translated from the Persian	17
	Chariots of desire	21
	Epitaph I and II	27
	Bulb	73
	Follow my lieder	90
	The case for late October	121
Kate Smith	Does nothing rhyme with Anthony?	37
Rob Stepney	Browing old, and bits and bobs	73
	About Blue	78
	Bad things were done in Ephesus	89
	An ABC of poetry	114
	When might time have stopped?	131
Ethel Thornett	Cissie Gomm	110
Tim Widdows	A Dad in a million	39
	Mums of the world	40
	Farewell Fiesta	92
	Jam and Jerusalem	118
Moira Wyatt	Footsteps	29
	Sleep love	35
	The portrait	86
	Christmas spirit	106
	Echoes of summer in Pazenas	107
	The school walk	109
Rosa Young	Sunset hours	32

I
Love and loss

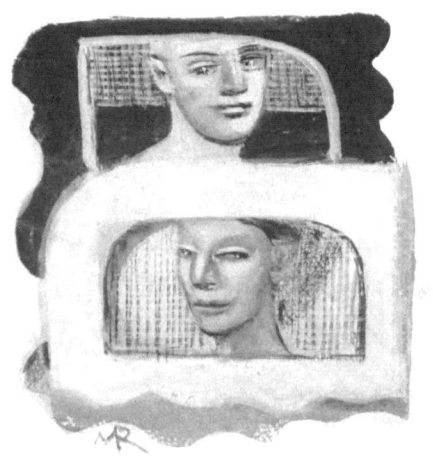

"… We swapped a smile, and one of those long looks
  That lodges like a splinter in the heart…"

¶ 14

A massage for my mother
Brigid Avison

I stroke your skin, so soft and tissue-fine.
How strangely unfamiliar to me,
Your body which when young enveloped mine.

My fingers trace each yielding, smooth decline.
Touched by your trust and vulnerability,
I stroke your skin, so soft and tissue-fine.

For years against you I my self defined,
Resisting, as a pebble might the sea,
Your body which when young enveloped mine.

But now I recognise just how benign
Your influence has been, to help me be,
I stroke your skin, so soft and tissue-fine.

Be gentle as you struggle to resign
Yourself to age, and use it tenderly,
Your body which when young enveloped mine.

One cord was cut, but stronger bonds now twine
Around our separate selves. Attached yet free,
I stroke your skin, so soft and tissue-fine -
Your body which when young enveloped mine.

The everyday moment
Anthony Landale

There is a great silence
Which I have slowly come to acknowledge
I cannot find without you.
It is a space where miracles occur
A place of emptiness
In which I disappear.
And in this great space time slows down
And I see how small and irresistibly full
Each moment is.
And all I have to do to be in this miracle
Is lean into this future with you
Listening wildly.
Daring to believe that it is always waiting
In its everyday way, right beside us.

Remind me to breathe
Mark Moss

Remind me to breathe.
Whisper it to me in cool mornings,
When envious Helios drags me from you

And I, tied to that bright chariot,
Am bid to toil, to chase him
Across the sky to twilight.

Tell me there, when our lips cling briefly
And the gift of your kiss leaves a promise of more,
Despite the sorrow of reluctant parting

There, when I am beguiled by a sleepy smile
And trapped by a cage of caresses,
Carried on remnant magic carpets

Drifting from lingering sleep
To dreams of rapturous embrace
Beyond the tug of a jealous sun,

There, in that moment that I forget
All but you,
Remind me to breathe.

As if translated from the Persian
Mick Rooney

Who am I?
As in a cloud of dust,
The great caravanserai
Passed by.
Take me with you!
Me. All day marking time
Milking goats.
And she! And she!
So proud. So proud.
Surrounded by her maids.
But she returned my gaze.
This she did.
And set the dust ablaze.
Take me with you!
But who am I?

My life, it changes
From woodsmoke to jasmine.
Oh God! That the air
Should take me,
And make me
Damask rose-
Spilled scent
To woo my love.

He worked himself
To a lover's pitch

Casting almonds
At his bride.
He knew not
What her lips were.
But still he loved her.
A bad fool, a mad fool.
A jester in disguise.

Peace of mind

Tim Crisp

You've been with me all my life,
And I don't want to lose you.
You've been a presence, a figurehead,
An example to follow. I've loved you,
Missed you, always admired you.
I see parts of you in my children
And that comforts me, it reassures me.
With them my heritage is entwined with your future
And it's looking good.
I hope your pain goes away, it is
Undeserved, and unfair. I would
Take it myself, if I could.
You know that I care, and I need
You to know what I think.
How can this moment be good, when we all
Struggle to face the ultimate truth?
But, more than anything, that is what I want.
Understand and know that we will
All be fine. We will be more than fine;
Much more. And that is because of you.

Blue Baby: I

Hilda Reed

Blue baby
Blue baby
Born with a veil
Sing to me
Sing to me now
Of the time

We loved.
Bodies ablaze in the frost-filled room,
bells cracking the icy air of the old year,
our flooding warmth impervious
to the brittle cold of night.

Then, in autumn, warm and golden,
you came;
a blue caul trailing vestiges
of winter past, of frost to come.

Your mother's hair, in soft, auburn waves,
rich as the autumn which brought you,
caught your fingers,
tangled your curling ear
and warmed you like the sun.

Blue Baby: II

In the blue-grey chill of dawn he came,
like a Delft bowl veiled in light,
the angles and curves of his face
softened by a caul.
My blue baby.

Now his laughter,
like lightning in an indigo night,
darkens my heart.
The blue-grey dawn chills my soul
and stills the life in my eyes.

A fine romance
Malcolm Gibb

Across a table selling tapes and books,
Just as the Street Fair made its stuttered start,
We swapped a smile, and one of those long looks
That lodges like a splinter in the heart.

Yet shy at this rich gaze, I fled away
To browse the slews of bric-a-brac: too proud
To speak. But, told his name and he was gay,
I looked for him again amid the crowd

And saw him there. And saw him with his friend.
And knew, as failing summer spattered rain,
I cannot bear beginnings for their end;
And could not brave the storm of love again.

Now cash is counted. Now the stalls are gone.
Now on the stage a band begins to jam
Discordantly; and life, unchanged, goes on
Save this: his face, now part of what I am.

High-rise loving
Bella Hewes

Wired for sound
fused with the air
our flat lies sprawled half-way to heaven.
Kaleidoscopes of sky-scapes by day
astonishing horizons.
An ocean of lights below by night
Occasionally a plane.

Curtains left open when we make love...
We are so high
only the angels observe us.

Chariots of desire

Mick Rooney

Beside the tins of mandarins
Her chariot is standing by.
Along the rows of Coca-Cola
I hear her give a mournful sigh.
I see her take a kitchen roll
And I, and I, and I, and I and I
I simply melt away.

She's choosing dark organic grapes
Their vineyard bloom her fingers rub
Along the shelves of beans and pulses
My heart's a chocolate bar in love
I see her take a kitchen roll
And I, and I, and I, and I, and I
I simply melt away.

Oh! Sweet chariot
Down the aisle she wheels in style
Oh! Sweet chariot
Take her where the checkout waits
Oh! Sweet chariot
Let me, Lord, be next in line
Let my Hobnobs, let them know
Their fate.

Beside the cuts of silverside
Past ciabatta oven fresh
To where green melons never ripen
Our trolleys touch in secret tryst
She puts a kitchen roll in mine
And I, and I, and I, and I, and I
I simply melt away.

Today we weigh pale chanterelles
And Spanish lemons, rind unwaxed
A meal for two, a chicken korma

Our passions poured from jumbo packs
I take a sheet of kitchen roll
And we, and we, and we, and we, and we
We simply melt away.

Oh! Sweet Harriet
Let us always stand in line
Oh! Sweet Harriet
Take us to the checkout till
Oh! Sweet Harriet
Packing now our bag for life
One credit card, one cash-back bill.

A Paraphrase of Horace's Ode "Vides ut alta…"

Elizabeth Llewellyn-Smith

On a cold December afternoon in Oxford, an elderly Fellow entertains and advises a handsome young undergraduate from the Junior Common Room.

Sharp frosts have made the streams stand still,
The snow lies thick on Cumnor Hill,
Bare branches crack beneath their load,
While we defy the wintry chill.

Pile on the logs and sit at leisure
Around the hearth in social pleasure;
Take from the rack a vintage wine
And pour it round in generous measure.

All else leave to the powers that be,
Who rule the gales, who calm the sea,
The storm-tossed branches come to rest
On cypress and on rowan tree.

Just take each day that comes, and greet
An asset in life's balance sheet.
Youngsters like you must not despise
Dances and dates and pop bands' beat.

At your age you can focus all
Your powers on bat and blade and ball,
On drinks in City dives and bars,
Events in College JCRs,
The assignation by the walls,
The giggling as the darkness falls;
The bangle snatched from off her wrist –
She scuffles but does not resist.

Lionel

Philip Drew

A great while ago his mother called to him,
"Lionel, Lionel. Come this way my darling."
He moved slowly through the hot morning air.
"Come quickly, my dear. Run, Leo, run."
He ran on the very tips of his toes
Scampering across the terrace.
"Oh Anya," his mother said. "Listen –
His feet make no more sound than the feet of a mouse."
He can remember how they laughed, the three of them –
Anya with her sharp white teeth, his mother and himself.
But what happened next he cannot remember.

There was a war. Or were there two wars?
Certainly there was a war,
But it was many years ago, and things have changed.
Where are they now, plump little Anya
And his mother, who always wore the softest of muslins?

At some point they went elsewhere,
And now one alone is left
To shuffle slowly across the terrace.
Did someone call, "This way, this way.
Hurry, Leo my lamb"?
Creeping with doubtful step towards the voice
And the faint fading scent of roses,
My feet make no more sound than the feet of a mouse.

Encounter

Jane Corbett

Last night I collided with a deer.
I was rounding the corner where the woods end
and the fields begin in the midnight dark.

She came bounding onto the road then stopped
irresolute, facing me in the headlights
she glanced and glanced again then leapt
straight on into my braking path.

Through the frame of the car
I felt her slender neck arch and crunch,
and something precious taken out of the night.

That side of midnight the road is just
a dead grey strip between two woods,
on the way to the places she goes.

Afraid of how easy it had been, I drove on.
But when I reached home I knew I had
to return and drove back.

She had been swept off the road, deposited in a ditch
by other cars, and in the glare of my headlamps
I saw her eyes clouded beyond doubt.

In the morning light as I drove down that road again
I saw that only flattened grass remained
where the white hump of her body had lain

And later found her wiry white hairs mixed up
in the crusted dirt on my car bumper.
I did not brush them off.

Tandem nursing

Kat Patrick

For nine months,
You'd waited …
Waited for the milk to return.
We cuddled,
Your new brother
Snuffling by my side.
You looked up
With two-year-old eyes
And tugged at the cross-wrapped pleat
Of mummy's nightgown.
New milk dribbled from your lips.
"Milky mi-mi," you gurgled,
And the baby coo'd.

Love's the meaning of life

Peter Head

Love a beautiful thing
It can make you cry
It can make you sing
It's nice two people can share
A whole life time together
Being there for each other
Forever and ever
Looking back
On some of the things they've done
Looking back to see
How far they've come
Given up your friends
Put your lives on hold
But the love you've found
Is worth much more than gold
Some people search a life time

For the things you've got
You have found the meaning of life
Where others have not
You'd give up your hearts
To be cut up and sold
As long as you've got each other
To cherish and to hold
You'd give it all never to be apart
Share a love share a heart
When you find someone
Hold on tight
Do the best for them
Do what's right
When you find someone
And they're your light
Think of each other
Try not to fight
Fight for them protect them be their best friend
And if they're in trouble be there till the end
You stand by them again and again
And if you're in trouble they'll do the same
I would like to dedicate this poem to
The most special and beautiful relationship I knew
Here's to endless love and constant care
The fun they've had and the laughs we shared
All the smiles and all the frowns
All the ups and all the downs
Each other's light at the end of the tunnel when things were dim
There for each other through everything
There for each other when things were grim
Supporting each other through thick and thin
It crept up and planted its seed and before we knew
The most wonderful plant called love grew
The first time they met their hearts raced
The love for each other can't be replaced
Their hearts race every time they meet
All the best in the future until the day we sleep

Feeding the wolf
Anthony Landale

Every night I dream that I am alone.
And you? You are not here.
I look for you and am bewildered.
I cannot run.
Haste clings to my legs.
I shout: "Are you hiding?
Or are you just ahead?"
I do not recognise where I am
And there is a hole
Where I used to feel connected.
I wake and look at you asleep.
My bag is packed
But I am not leaving.
I am just feeding the wolf
And howling at the moon.

Epitaph I
Mick Rooney

Who this night rattles the reeds
To start the bittern's boom?
Another soul passing through.
A smile, surprised that it was so.
That she should go before her time.
Alright! But not like this – broken
By the roadside.
No room for air on the acrid breeze.
Only the rattle of the reeds,
Her death.
And all the while
A fenland bittern boomed
The night away.

Epitaph II

We do smile
That they had no fame.
And we weep at their passing.
Yet something more remains.
Many they were
Who filled the breach
Along the line.
Entrenched in earth they lie.
Deep the furrows
From the plough
Seagulls follow,
Lapwings too.
Golden youth – all dead.
And true, we weep.
Yet we do smile.
For though they had no fame
Still they do remain.

A good soldier

John Lanyon

Tales of you walking in the high hills
Of Kashmir and Kilimanjaro
Trading jewels in the market place
Riding in your armoured car across the desert
Fixing the engine in the dark
Checking the time on your Rolex Oyster
Capturing the proudest tribesmen
With your battered Leica
Catching huge silver-bellied fish by the lakeside
Exchanging words in Hindi, Punjabi, Arabic, Swahili

7883943, Sergeant Lanyon
I salute you and ask

What strategy decided
That you would die
Without grammar
In your wheelchair tank
From some mysterious internal war?

Footsteps

Moira Wyatt

The invalid lay and listened
All day and every day
Lying on pillows white as snow
Beneath a bedspread gay.

Her cheeks were pale as lilies white
Her hair a chestnut mane.
Her eyes were full of quiet light
That hid her constant pain.

She lay and listened all day long
To all the steps that passed
And to the birds' free joyous song
Until night came at last.

She knew each footstep well by heart
She knew who she must greet
She often gave her friends a start
Saying their name before they meet.

The Doctor – heavy-footed man,
With measured even pace,
The Nurse, who used to be her nan,
Who ran a silent race.

The Maid who shuffled, sniffing, past,
Bearing her heavy trays,
The Minister whose footsteps fast
Flew round his flock on certain days.

But never came the footsteps she longed
And listened for, all day
The steps that meant the world to her –
At last would show the way.

They came one night from out the dark,
Slow treading, firm and sure,
As they nearer came and came
They had a strange allure

At last! At last, such sweet release!
No more of silent pain.
He comes! He brings me lasting peace,
Oh Death – long may he reign

Requiem
Robert Macefield

Echoes of light
Upon an empty stage
The book, frowning,
Turns its own page

A cast of millions
Grease paint and dried blood
Heartbreak, no to love
Where structures once stood

Without power
A projector cranks its own film
A screen flickers white light
Panavision
Empty seats between realities
And fiction knows not division

Who to see
Who to be seen

Except the turnings of a machine?

The book, understanding,
Steps from its page

An echo of light... upon the stage
Takes a bow
And leaves its gilded

Cage

Our loss
Peter Head

Put on a lone flower
And your only black dress
Meet at the church
To lay a friend to rest
Even though everyone hurts
I had to go along
And say my bit in the church
So here's to you
You're one of a kind
Not a day goes by
When you're not on our mind
I'm trying to hold it in
Losing weight, looking thin
I'm trying to hold it back
Too late I click and snap
You killed yourself out of spite
Now we're lost in the fading light
Upsetting feelings spoken aloud
In a church to quite a crowd
Whatever was going through your head?
The day you died our hearts bled
Whatever was going through your brain?
Lost the plot, going insane

Whatever was going through your heart?
One minute you're here then you part
Whatever was going through your head?
Wasn't there something I could have said?
I guess if it had been better here
You would have stayed
Drinking beers and getting laid
And as you bring us to our knees
More to look forward to
They say death comes in threes
Shut yourself off to it, don't get hurt
Funeral Friday blazer and shirt
And even though everyone cries
I had to go along and say my goodbyes
Forgotten gravestone, feel alone
Forgotten gravestone laced in moss
You've gone, our loss

Sunset hours

Rosa Young

As Autumn leaves will gently lose their hold
Fluttering from trees at closing of the year
So shall my life, like nature, reach its end
And loosen bonds with those I hold most dear.

Faces I love will need no mourning gloom
The burden of tearful sadness they are spared
Rather the golden memories and gratitude
For the joyous family of a lifetime shared.

It may be that there is another world
But if not I will gladly lie
Beneath the fallen leaves and lovely flowers
And join the world of nature when I die.

Last respects
Eileen Dore

Who's that standing by my grave?
Oh yes, it's that Mrs Price –
And another woman from up my street
Come to pay their respects – how nice!

"She'll be sadly missed," I hear one say
"A good woman, one of the best!"
The other nods, and bows her head
"Oh blessed, yes, truly blessed!"

Back and forth the praises flow
For the woman who once was me.
I flush with pride, my wings turn pink
What a paragon I used to be!

I hover as they both bend down
Floral tributes to peruse.
Puzzled, I hear a muffled laugh –
Words of sympathy shouldn't amuse!

"This isn't Doris lying here.
I'd heard this one died the same day.
Come on, I never did like her.
Good riddance is all I can say!"

Charlie's demise
Eileen Dore

Wotcher – you – how bist then you?
What's that thee got on thee y'ead?
Thee best 'at dids't say
Will wot's up today?
D'unt tell I that somebody's j'ead!
No chent ol' Charlie who's kicked the buckut?

Will sorry that I be
How old was the poor ol' devil?
No he wuzn't ninetythree?
And it wuzn't natural causes?
Well go on, tell I more –
Wot, thee says he died of lead poisoning
Administered by the widder next door!
Her said they'd an understandin' –
And one day 'oped to be wed.
But when her went to Charlie's t'uther evening
Her found sumbody else in his bed!
Well, thee cud'st knock I down with a feather!
Charlie wuz a dark 'orse that's for sure,
Spruz he fancied summat a bit younger –
The widder being ninetyfour!
That yent the way it wuz, thee says?
Her udn't a minded if that wuz true
Reason widder blasted 'im wuz
T'other 'umman was a hundred and two!

True voice

Anthony Landale

Have you noticed that nobody is going to save you?
Even though you keep on believing they will.
But even God doesn't want that responsibility.
And I? I'd rather have you in a thousand pieces
Than staying small – waiting for a day
When you give yourself permission to stand tall.
To speak with your true voice.
To be the person you always hoped you'd become.

Sleep love
Moira Wyatt

Sleep love,
And rest your silky
Hair against my cheek.
Sleep love,
And fling your passionate
Limbs to rest.
Sleep love,
And press your beating heart
To mine.
Sleep love,
And twine yourself as one
With me.
Sleep love,
And know not that my hands
Explore your face:
Sleep love,
Sleep with me.

Love
Dee Moss

How do I love you? Cannot count the ways
Since first we met in bomb-scarred London church.
Through seven long years of scribbled words by post
Until the day, in that same re-built church,
We made our vows – I promised to obey!
We also vowed to God that we would love Him
As we loved each other.
Soon there was more loving in our lives,
Three lively sons, who filled our busy days
With joy and laughter. There was also work.
At first we had no car, TV or heated house.
You were appalled by my cold feet in bed.
But these were happy times.

Then moving days.
We went from town to town,
Five times we made new friends but through it all
Our best friend was each other.
Then sorrows came, yet never overcame
The faith we shared, and the true knowledge
Of the love of God.

Now we are old, but never once in all these sixty years
Have we parted with a hurtful word.
We've had our quarrels and you still complain
About cold feet upon your legs in bed.
But through it all, the smiles, the aching tears,
I will still love you, to the end of time.

Colouring in literature

John Lanyon

She bestows the day-glo,
Luminous acid-green for character,
Fluorescent baby-pink for plot,
Safety-jacket yellow for irony.

These are the important bits,
Workmanlike,
Like editing "Match of the Day",
Like colouring counties, rainfall distribution,
Oil deposits.

This is Act One.

Compare and Contrast
The toddler's disrespect for boundaries,
Fat crayons in tiny hands
Cross the thick black lines
Of cheap and cheerful colouring books.

I want to respect her.

It's nostalgia
For the first meeting with a text,
Something with something to say,
For being 17.

"The Highlighter Pen –
The Beginning of Postmodernism? – Discuss"
City blocks of colour
Over tenant words,
Uncompromising urban renewal,
Double-glazing for Mr Larkin,
A suburban lawn for Mr Hughes.

Young and pretty,
She's written her name in the front
Easy with literature,
The way I never was.

Does nothing rhyme with Anthony?

Kate Smith

Surely there's a gentle word, brown, or maybe corduroy,
Smelling of fresh grass, or wrestling with a lawnmower,
That rhymes with Anthony?

A green word, sometimes blue, that plays a subtle melody
Of interweaving harmony, occasional cacophony
That rhymes with Anthony

Perhaps it is a quirky word of shades and contradictions
Like 'shall' or 'shan't' or 'can' or 'can't' on each
and every turn
To rhyme with Anthony

No, more a true and thoughtful word, of friendship and of constancy
Of tennis, bridge and family – (revoking's a calamity)
that rhymes with Anthony

A river rhyme of waterside, a writer's flow of poetry
Blue kingfisher darting words, canoes and swans, catastrophe
Arranged to rhyme with Anthony

In fact the word that's Anthony
Is quite unique, it stands alone
No other words quite magnify that quality of Anthony
Maybe that's why there is no word
That can ever rhyme with Anthony

Written as a 50th birthday tribute.

Labour report (and bits about potatoes)

John Lanyon

Saturday morning. Wet. The pregnant seed potatoes make it from the damp, plastic carrier bag to the egg trays in the new baby's room. (The variety, Epicure.) This is almost spring!

In the greengrocer's that morning every one seemed to know you had had a show. Their potatoes promise little – it's been a bad year for potatoes.

Twinges. A gobbled lunch of simple food (no potatoes – they deserve lots of time). We couldn't find the pink book. (It tells you when to go to the hospital.) Relief as you find it under knitting-patterns.

We drive to the hospital in my brother's car. He's on holiday in France. I wonder which potato varieties they grow there. We find a parking place. (I was worried we wouldn't and would have to go back home.)

The seismograph records your belly-quakes – could it really be you'll be another Sumo wrestler out of a job? I marked Third Year exam papers. You have a feminist novel. I read *Midnight's Children.* Television. Peasants in France. Peter Maxwell Davies talks about his Third Symphony. A woman wanders by, listens keenly, the music does not connect. She telephones.

Another room. Something is happening. You don't want me to laugh. Be there! Our breath starts the long, slow double concerto. Tell Max. We go downstairs. It is just after midnight and cleaners and porters and tea-makers are abroad. We meet our midwife. We were almost neighbours. I almost knew her husband. We like her. She wears a chain of the thinnest gold. No crucifix. A second movement to our double concerto. The theme, no common riff, this, is stated, amplified, elaborated and restated. It grows in intensity. The midwife conducts a little but gives the soloist room to explore. I play second fiddle. Time after time. You go *sforzando fff*. The soloist plays her cadenza. Her perineum swells like a massive orange. The baby is there. It's a boy.

The Sumo wrestler is gone. Your stomach is like an old potato. So it goes. A new contestant steps into the ring. New music.

A dad in a million
Tim Widdows

A dad in a million,
Yes that's what you are,
My personnel chauffeur,
With executive car.

My private banker,
This one I can trust,
He charges no interest,
And doesn't care if I'm bust.

He's an odd job man,
With talents galore,
Just give him a shout,
No job is too small.

Every child shouts aloud,
Yes my dad's the best!
But he has a beer belly,
And wears a string vest.

A movie star was always his calling,
The times we've heard that, it's getting quite boring,
Fighting the baddies and kissing the girl,
But he's more like our Brucie, now give us a twirl.

For you, Dad, this day was made
To show how much we care
But if we told you what we really think,
It might just make you swear.

Happy Fathers' Day

(To be read in the style of Pam Ayres)

Mums of the world
Tim Widdows

What would we do without Mum?
At times she's a pain in the bum!
If nagging was a sport,
She'd have a glowing report,
And think it's all part of the fun.

Now mums think always they're right,
And love to put up a fight.
They always know best
And say sod to the rest
I wish my kids were this bright.

There's times we needed our mum
Like the scratch on the knee
When we fell out that tree
Or the door that slammed on your thumb

And do you remember the meals?
How queasy they made us all feel.
Now eat up your Brussels

They'll give you big muscles
Just like the carrots and peas.

So to all the mums in the world
Your kids just want to be sure.
That if they had the pick of the bunch
We'd like the one next door!

(To be read in the style of Pam Ayres)

Inheritance

Margery Mayhew

Now, Mother dear, do be seated
We think a long, frank talk is needed

This house is large, a move is due
A sheltered flat is best for you

Also, dear mother, we'll need to know
About "arrangements" when you go

Think it over and remember, do
We only want what's best for you

So mother, when she went to bed
Thought it over, as they had said

She sold the house, spent the money
Cruised the world, tasted the honey

She stayed away, a long, long time
Flirting with officers of the Cunard line

The "arrangements" were her own.
She was buried at sea, so never went home.

Decisions
Margery Mayhew

Amo, Amas, Amat
I love you, love you, love you
But you don't like my cat
He makes you sneeze
He makes you wheeze
He ruins our gaudy moments
And we really can't have that

You say forever
You will love me, love me, love me
You promise to love no other
But I am not so green
This is a different scene
One more sneeze
One more wheeze
You will leave me for another

So I'll settle for the cat.
While there is tuna in the larder
Central heating in the flat
He will stay, never stray
As we both grow old and grey
And if he dies before I do
I'll get another cat!

Three more weeks to go
Rebecca Collins

Three more weeks to go.
Before we have to leave
To live two hours from here.
Soon too far away
For trips to the swings
Via the Co-op for bread
Or the library for new books
While visiting the pharmacy
And the post office to send a card
To Archie, that is, 'cousin' Archie

Three more weeks to go.
No more Preschool for us.
'Get your shoes on! Quick!'
Trudging up The Slade
'I'm tired, mummy.' (You try pushing this then!)
Lifting children to look at the stream
Squeezing the pushchair past wheelie bins
Searching for black plimsolls in a lake of the same
Small-talk about nappies, sleep and food.
None of that now

Three more weeks to go.
Why are we moving, remind me?
Listening to next door's cockerel
Waking me up in the morning
Followed by number two son
Poking me in the face: 'Is it time to get up yet?'
What shall we do today?
Let's just go to the swings again.
We are leaving Charlbury.
We need our heads seeing to.

¶ 44

II
River and stone

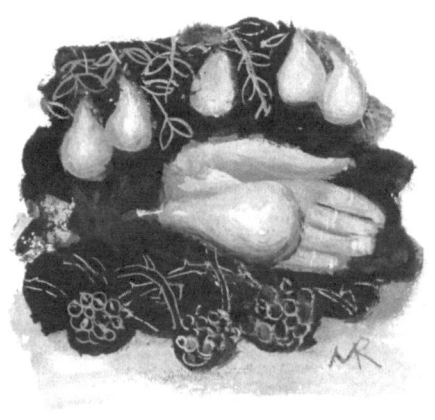

*"… And gather fruits and feverfew
From heath and hedgerow daubed with dew…"*

¶ 46

A walk in winter
In memoriam Jean Westley

Hilda Reed

Sunlight on the flooded field
revealed the heavy beak; the briar
higher than the flood, displayed
the radiant richness of the bird:
the unexpected kingfisher.

Shadows lengthened,
air cooled,
colour drained
from bird and briar.

Without a word we watched until
the stillness broke: electric blue
it flew a flashing sunlit arc,
sparking a sudden joy, to fill
the void, the ebbing day, with life.

Dreams of Mother Evenlode

Mark Moss

Because we never said goodbye,
You meander through my dreams,
Burbling around my sharp-edged days
With your shallow lullaby,
Smoothing them in your caress
Before dropping them to your pebbled bottom
As you swallow their ripples.

You cradle me, Mother Evenlode,
Just as dace and tench
Find shelter beneath the shadows
Of bountiful blackberry, or bulrush,
Or fingers of summer-laden willows,

Wary of your kingfishers:
Royal blue proclamations of birthright
In a land of monarchs,
Set above a red blush
Of apology
To the fishes.

You are my church pew,
My sanctuary,
My sleep-vault of memories:

Laughter chasing lazy puffs of gnats
Through time-locked August days;

The bitter sting of thorn and nettle,
Soothed by the sweet taste of berry;

Or an orange-tipped float
Drifting across your clear smile,
Unmolested by lazy squatters.

Good Mother.
You whisper your truths
On the ragged edge of my dreams:
"Ignore them.
I will make them pebbles, Charlbury son.

Summers yet remain for us.

Remember the greenwood,
And the call of pheasant
Through the nectar-scent of cut hay.

Remember how your laughter floated
On the slow drift of time,
And the peace,
And that you can always return,

Because we never said goodbye."

Beating the bounds
Ian Colville

By oak and ash and old elm tree,
With laugh and song and merriment,
To beat the bounds of Charlbury,
The children went, the children went

By many a hawthorn-bordered lane,
With merriment, with laugh and song
Into the woods and out again,
They danced along, they danced along

With bluebells and with columbine,
With water lilies from the pool,
With orchises and eglantine,
Their hands were full, their hands were full.

Through buttercups and meadowsweet,
They made a road, they made a road,
Until their pollen-powdered feet
Came dancing to the Evenlode.

Ah! Do you know that silent stream,
The Evenlode, it runs so deep?
The Evenlode, its waters dream,
It seems asleep, it seems asleep.

Of jack and bream, the still abode
Haunt of the glittering dragonfly,
The willow-bordered Evenlode
Where kingfishers go flashing by.

The boat was ready on the brink,
They crowded in, they crowded in,
How could so light a cargo sink?
Tears end what laughter doth begin.

Their dance is stopped, their song is sped.
To flow as you have always flowed
With these three little flounderers dead,
Oh cruel, cruel Evenlode.

Where lilies through its waters hail
And o'er the darkling pool resounds
The non-impassioned nightingale,
And those small spirits beat the bounds.

(Published in the Charlbury Chronicle in 1999, this poem refers to the tragedy of 1924 in which three children died when a punt overturned while attempting to cross the Evenlode near Walcot during the annual walk around the parish boundary. It was found among papers left by Reg Leighton. We have been unable to trace Ian Colville.)

Does nothing rhyme with Charlbury?

Something does
Angus Bentall

A gardener, called Karl, lived in Charlbury
And he loaded his fruit plot with marl, for he
'd heard it on 'Wogan',
"Cross Tayberry with Logan."
 Success! A new hybrid – the Karlberry.

Rhyme
Dorothy Day

Does nothing rhyme with Charlbury?
Well, I can only think of mulberry.

Charlbury, a little town of stone,
In which mulberries are not grown.
You could be excused for thinking it's a weed,
But it's a tree on which silkworms feed.
How do I know this? I looked in a dictionary.
In the Mediterranean it grows extensively.
It's also a code name for an artificial harbour
Used in Europe in the Second World War.

Limerick

Leah Fowler

There was a young lady from Charlbury
Who said that she lived in a strawberry
The bards of the time
Said nothing would rhyme
With a quaint little town known as Charlbury

(Note for non-residents: the town's name is frequently pronounced "Chawbury".)

What rhymes with Charlbury?

Dee Moss

On the first month of New Year, we came to Charlbury.
We found four Christian churches,
One busy surgery,
Two careful dentists,
To care for health and spirituality.

On the next month of '08, we came to Charlbury,
Finding one lively art club,
Another for the gardeners,
Several for the young ones,
And a superb public library.

On the first month of springtime, we came to Charlbury.
We found one useful bookshop,
A garage selling fresh meat,
A news shop serving coffee,
And the new-look Co-op pharmacy.

On the first month of summer, we came to Charlbury,
Finding many sporty people,
Keen and active walkers,
And CADS, a drama group,
Whose players we all love to see.

On the first week of autumn, we came to Charlbury,
Spying many lovely gardens,
Lush grass on the Playing Close,
Several neat allotments,
And gardeners working merrily.

On the first week of Advent, we came to Charlbury,
Finding one busy Post Office,
Lots of kindly people,
Christmas trees on buildings,
And many folk supporting charity.

These Feet

Mark Moss

Tattered, twice-worn trainers
marked me, though I tried
to hide the hand-me-down
holes over wedge-worn soles
of shoes one size too big,
and not-quite-the-right-fit,
but good enough for a Sturt Close lad.

They were mirages, elusive
illusions of the idyll lying
at the edge of Wychwood,
the edge of Cornbury,
in whose rich muck I left
my ill-fitted prints.

You traced my tracks
down the length of your nose,
deaf to the plight of foot fighting leather.
Did you hear my hunger
over the roar of your protests
as I scrumped your orchards
of fruit you would rather see rot?

Grasping for masks
I nicked a name.
You knew Yorkie, but who
knew Mark? Who knew the path
these feet would find
when this Town of Stone grew
too tight for shoes you gave me?

Three green stripes, my ersatz
trademark—you saw prison bars,
a dole line, an unkempt grave.
Blind, you missed the good
father, graduate, the writer
hidden behind the rude patois
by which you marked me.

Would you know me today?
Would you welcome me home?
Knowing the distance
between the me of then and now
is the same whether trod
in your shoes, or those
good enough for a Sturt Close lad.

Dry stone walls
Igor Goldkind

You can't build a wall round a village.
You can try.
You can stack honeyed stone upon stone, fashion judgement upon judgement,
Into a long pretty barrier of decorative limestone,
To keep the outsiders out and the insiders in.
But you can't build a wall round a village.
The sun and the wind will always find their way in.

You can't build a wall round a village.
You can try.
You can hoist one po-faced block upon another, fit propriety to propriety;
Smooth over the sides to hide irregular shapes and push the pale, jagged ones in.
You can round your vowels and cluck your tongues,
You can suck your teeth and roll your plums,
You can forget where your grandparents come from or where your children are now loitering.
But you can't build a wall round a village.
The sun and the wind will always find their way in.

You can't build a wall round a village and pray the invaders go around.
Because they won't.
They'll be curious in their strange, slippery tongues
Which they'll cheerfully slip between the slits in your stones
Leaving the wet marks of our accents and the smells of strange foods behind
While still wondering what your wall was hiding all this time.
No, you can't build a wall round a village.
The sun and the wind will always find their way in.

You can't build a wall round a village.
You can try.
And when the quarries are all emptied of the stones you have taken,

You can always bake cakes to raise a few more,
Until the wall nearly buckles under its own sanctimony,
Stretched all the way from the private ground to the guarded gates of heaven,
Leaving only a slash of blue sky between the shadows of avarice and suspicion that darken your green.
You can worship the past as a paradise lost and dread the future: an uncertain hell.
But you can't build a wall round a village.
No, you can't:
The sun and the wind will always find their way in.

You can't build a wall round a village.
You can try.
You can bury your heroes under shovelfuls of piety while deporting the victims of wars;
Hide their sad faces behind the polite smiles you've carved into your church doors.
You can turn and press your face to the wall and call it Tolerance, if you choose
But it's Jericho not Jerusalem you've built on this mud,
And it's acceptance not tolerance, the lamb cries out for now.

No, you can't build a wall round a village.
But you can try.
Until your children and theirs grow as tall as the wall that surrounds them.
Their hands grown long and sharp enough, to claw at the stones of their prison.
From the inside out, they will tear your wall down;
To the let the sun and the wind and the outside in,
They will tear it down.
While your bones of contention lie long crumbled and buried in the graveyard by the wool church door.

You can't build a wall round a village.
The sun and the wind will always find their way in.
And sometimes the river will too.

England
Patricia Perry

In the country the autumn is glowing
Spreading through the fields like fire,
Rippling through the canopy of leaves,
Turning the green to red
And the gold to the crisp dry leaves
That lie crunching beneath our feet.

In the country the autumn is growing
And the first sharp mornings bring
Golden cobwebs glistening in the grass.
Children roll themselves over the stone walls
And fly across the September fields
Looking for blackberries behind stinging nettles and thorns.
Along the lane goes a horse and rider
Passing elderberries and crab apples high in the hedge.

In the country the autumn is growing,
Yielding herself to the last mellow embrace of the sun,
Sinking within her present consciousness,
Meditating,
And the silent spirits of the earth
Beckon one to the holy places
Where all life is silent and still.

Fog wraps the winter land,
And the copper fronded floor lies soft
Beneath the trees;
The curling wisps of mist creep
Over the blackberry and the old man's beard
And the last hips fall.

When the winter world lies breathing
And all the horizon is mountain peaks and snow
And the valleys are lost in mist and fog
One measures the proportion of man to the earth –
The passionless earth,

Endlessly creating life
In every second of the centuries' times,
Flowers, trees, insects, birds, animals and humans
In all their myriad forms.

All the peoples of the earth,
Who have been striving and achieving over the years,
Progressing from the point of their beginning
Through alternating cycles of culture and barbarism
With their different customs, religious rites
And strange histories,
What is now their future?

But there –
There's what matters most,
There's my England
Where the mist parts
And the land is green,
In the woodland where
Down all the long tempestuous centuries of Englishmen
The spirits dance unseen -
Dance in the silence
The sweet, green, cool, soft silence
Of the ever-growing earth.

O Charlbury Fish Van, Charlbury Fish Van, where art thou Charlbury Fish Van?

Adrian Lancini

For six long years I've searched the chartered streets of Charlbury
Driven on by hearsay, gossip and Chinese whispers
I've hunted for fresh halibut, scallops and kippers

I've frequented pubs
The playground of the rumour
But talk there was of speed humps and cricket
Not mackerel and tuna

An informer from Crawborough
Told me his niece from Ticknell Piece
Had seen the van outside the Co-op
So there I hurried
But all I found
Was a tied up hound
And a herd of youths in hooded tops and baggy jeans
Not a sniff of cockles, sea bass or langoustines

I withdrew my disappointment
And chased up on further leads
Sightings of cod and haddock
in Wychwood Paddocks
Of jellied eels
on Nine Acres fields
Of salmon terrine
by The Green
And fillet of shark
near Cornbury Park
But alas…

…they were all red herrings

Desperate, I dialled 118 118
Fishing for a number
But for 'Fish Vans in Charlbury'
Nothing came under

I Googled, Yahooed and even asked Jeeves
But links to a campsite in Swansea
Was all I received

Then it came to me...of course
The clue was in the name
If the van would stop anywhere
It must be Fishers Lane

Over seven days and seven nights
I sat there through wind and rain
A resilient fisherman riding a storm
My catch would be worth my pain

But the only van that passed, those seven days and seven nights
Contained nothing from the seas
The only van to pass me
Was detecting TVs

On a grey and chilly Tuesday, I decided to abandon ship
And with sorrows to drown
I shuffled myself forlornly
Towards The Rose and Crown

But as I arrived and the church bells chimed thrice
The sun appeared with one last roll of the dice
Shining down on a smiling man
Stood proudly, behind a gleaming white van
And there, he bestowed upon my outstretched hands
A tail of monkfish and a bag of clams

My prayers had finally been answered
I'd been granted my wish
I'd found the van in Charlbury
That stops to sell us fish

Rain, rain, go away

Peter Barber

Water, so we were taught, finds its own level:
We can go along with that.
Air of course is another matter
Birds seem to have got the knack
Of using it to their advantage.
And so have we; flying is now, if not our first,
Our second nature. To soar is human, to arrive divine.
But whoever heard of windhover falling heart failing
To earth, because of engine trouble?

Water however, as we know, finds its own level.
And fish take to it swimmingly.
In cold blood we follow them, not quite in our element,
Progress requires grasp and gasp.
We can just manage it, though
Through pipe and duct -
Retained, contained by wall, mole, and barrage.
We master it then, needing the force that it supplies.
But, as we know, water finds its own level.
Unforeseen, unimaginable.

Rain, rain, go away
Come again another day.

The Great Flood
Rebecca Collins

My son still remembers
The day we were flooded.
It wasn't when you think.
It was a year before that:
We were lucky last year
And unlucky the year before.

It all happened so fast.
I tried to stop it coming.
'It's raining' said my son.
'No, really?' I wanted to scream
The house was not the same
I really hate the rain

The cat didn't notice,
She stayed away all day.
She didn't like the aftermath:
Her bowl floating in water.
We had to move out for the summer
Refugees while the house recovered

Now I can't stand the rain.
I stand on the step and watch.
I listen to the sound on the roof
And my son still remembers.
'Perhaps it will flood again' he says.
'I hope not,' is all I can say

Oxfordshire 2007

Keith Fountain

Keep the sun behind you and you'll
Reach Sibford, Horton and Balscote.
There are the oaks, the sycamores,
The horse chestnuts, tall against the northern sky,
Winding the lanes in case you miss them.

You can see further in the south, across the broad valleys,
But this year the rivers snapped walls and gates like twigs,
Drowning cars and chickens. The damp straw still clings to
the wire, alien corn from the west, threaded by the flood.

How could gentle weaving sit beside such power?

I'll go north next year with a backward glance,
Listening for the sound of water.

(Keith Fountain, who lives in Australia, is a regular visitor to Charlbury. This poem first appeared in the Charlbury Chronicle.)

In Finstock Field

Gareth Miller

Oh, how I love September days,
These hazy, lazy, crazy days.
Oh, how I love to wander through
These woodland ways and fields of maize,
And lie beneath the balmy blaze
In harvest's stubble residue,
And bathe my soul in skies of blue
And feel that faith at last is true.

Oh, how I love September days,
This crazy, hazy, lazy phase.
Oh, how I love to tiptoe through
This mossy maze, these shady bays,

And glimpse the sun's reclining rays
On leafy limbs of oak and yew,
And rest my heart in autumn's hue,
Recharged by nature's retinue.

Oh, how I love September days,
These carefree lack-a-daisy days.
Oh, how I love to rendezvous
With heaven in Finstock's avenue,
And gather fruits and feverfew
From heath and hedgerow daubed with dew,
And sing a song of heartfelt praise,
Which winter's blight shall not erase.

He dwells in the ground of my being
Jenifer Brown

Because I am in need of grace
God sends a lark,
Who makes her nest where it is quiet,
Within my dark.

With loving care she'll line the place
Of ancient hate;
The most primeval part of me,
Gently domesticate.

Above her head will kindnesses
Like flowers, grow.
The clover and the meadowsweet
His glory show.

Down through the earth, their slender roots
Gently invade
The delicate and hidden place,
Which she has made.
But oh! My pride turns up the stones,
Choking instead

The clover and the meadowsweet.
Buttercups, dead.

My cruelties are pebbles sharp
Striking below.
My envies and my vanities
Like brambles grow.

I must go out and free the ground
Of thorns and pain;
Subdue the substance of the soil
To peace again.

Then, when I take the Bread and Wine
And all is done
She mounts – she mounts – singing,
Into the sun.

Port Meadow

Gareth Miller

Here all the properties of health and peace combine,
Here things of earth with things of heaven entwine;
Sky, wind and sun betray a celestial source,
While waves and water weave an earthbound course.

Here near the city's heart a magic place survives,
Here an oasis while the city strives;
Noise and necessity do not annoy or jar,
And gentle streams meander near and far.

Here I can breathe away my passions and my pains,
Here I can soothe and dissipate the strains;
Horses and walkers mingle; cows, ducks and geese converge,
And nature's comeliness erases every urge.

Charlbury's full of ceorls
Mark Moss

Charles, now this is silly stuff,
You're now amongst the rude and rough,
And though you've roots near Marylebone,
You summer in this town of stone.

Used to servants' bobbing heads,
You tried to stop our church bells dead,
And failed. You then did check your aim
Against our burgh's beguiling name.

Now, we who drew a meaner lot
Must make a peace with 'wot we got',
For in your low regard we rate
Nowt-all but council-poor estates.

But ask how your second home
Did grow from Cotswold honey stone.
'Twas not May's hand, nor tired Brunel's
That set our little town so well.

A pearl, an ancient Lord bestowed
To Ceorls upon the Evenlode,
A point that you, so lately came,
So churlishly deny, for shame!

A Sturt Close lad will set you straight,
When history falls to fell debate
That sound as pounds, and bright as pearls,
The truth is Charlbury's full of Ceorls.

In Charlbury town
Hilda Joy Jones

In Charlbury town, in Charlbury town
The people walk up, the people walk down
Saying "Good morning. How do you do?"
In Charlbury town, people greet you.

In Charlbury town, in Charlbury town
Children run up, children run down,
Onto Nine Acres, running about
Swing on the swings, play games and shout,
Playing football, and tennis too,
Children in Charlbury, that's what they do.

In Charlbury town, in Charlbury town
There are lots of shops to shop around.
Post office, chemist, bookshop too,
News and Things, Good Food Shop,
Pleased to serve you.
There's the Co-op and Fiveways,
Hairdressers two
Use them or lose them,
It's up to you!

The people we know
Rebecca Collins

The postman who always wears shorts
He knocks really loudly.
The lady with the big black dogs
She walks past every day.
The noisy teenagers next door
Running up and down the stairs.
The man with the Christmas lights
Letting me read in bed.
The smiley lady in the Co-op
Chatty, however big the queue.

The man with the big white moustache
Looking like a lost army general.
The lady jogging up the Slade
Swaying hair down past her bottom.
I wonder if any of these people
Have a sentence to say about me.

Charlbury's contrasting worlds
Bella Hewes

The computer now shut down,
I escape the virtual world
Looking for peace and refreshment.

A prance of purple foxgloves
A ten foot thrust of thistle
A canter of clover
A tall dark huddle of giant hog-weed
The unexpected sudden sweet scent of high-up honeysuckle
And even higher, the roar of the grey bomber going back to Brize Norton.

Then, a sizzle of stitchwort
A swim of pink campion
A dance of daisies
A stately stroll of nettles
A riot of dog-rose
And above me, an explosion of noise, the black stealth bomber cruises the skies.

Thankfully,
A merry festival of meadow fescue
A glow of dandelions
A bliss of buttercups
A tangle of white bryony
A banter of has-been bluebells
And much too close, a khaki hedge-hopping helicopter
"Looking for the local rapist", I am reliably informed.

I return gratefully to the peace of my double-glazed dwelling.

III
Shorts

*"…Health, Music, Wine, Laughter, Silence,
Together; how about it?…"*

Sarah Geeson-Brown

Walcot illuminations

In the writer's bed
The open leaves of a book
And the cold white sheets

I begin each day
With porridge, tea and honey
While sheep bleat sadly

The Walcot lane is
Singularly embracing
A fox cries murder

Time is Even now
Nicked from Christina's pale hand
Blue enjoys his Tryst

Arthur Crisp

The Hardships of the 1995 North Berwick Grail

(a golf tournament)

Oh to be in Suffolk
Now that June has come
Or, failing that,
The urban copse
Of gentle Wimbledum.

Art

The shapes we sculpt
are extensions of the mind;
our fourth dimension.

Love

Reach out and touch me.
I am here; come and find me
so that I can give.

With you entwined,
I surrender my body
and share my mind.

Hold my heart gently,
your eyes smile tenderly through
moments blown by time.

Us

We are our parents
And express their bond; please let
us be fulfilled.

Immortality

Parents die; at last
we know their love and find our-
selves. So live the dead.

Survival

To live with sadness
is the greatest strain; that is
how mankind can grow.

Four Aces and the King of Spades

Truth, Knowledge, Love,
Health, Music, Wine, Laughter, Silence,
Together; how about it?

Mick Rooney

Bulb

He has grazed at the margins of culture.
This week he chews on Walt Whitman's beard,
And spits out "I sing America Electric",
Or some such rushed illumination.
But after five minutes, he's back in the dark.

Rob Stepney

Browing old gracefully

There comes a time when eyebrow tufts
Grow at an unsettling angle to the rest;
And you must settle to a Life of Dennis Healey.

Beyond Newton's laws

A definition of entropy that's true, if difficult to express in maths:
The force of children at work in the universe
No thing or feeling will ever be in its accustomed place

If I love you a million, it's seven letters
And seven figures, and two syllables, or maybe three;
But if I love you to the top of the stars, it's infinity

Paradox

My materialism is held as stubbornly as any sheep
Sticks to mountain ground. If you don't believe me,
I'll come back to haunt you

In praise of friction

It makes the wheels go round,
While things go in and out.
And so the race continues.

Badminton

You are like a flower, attentive to the sky;
Or clock, ticking your head as the shuttlecock tocks by.
How did we ever have a child so beautiful?

IV
Pastimes: the Colour Supplement

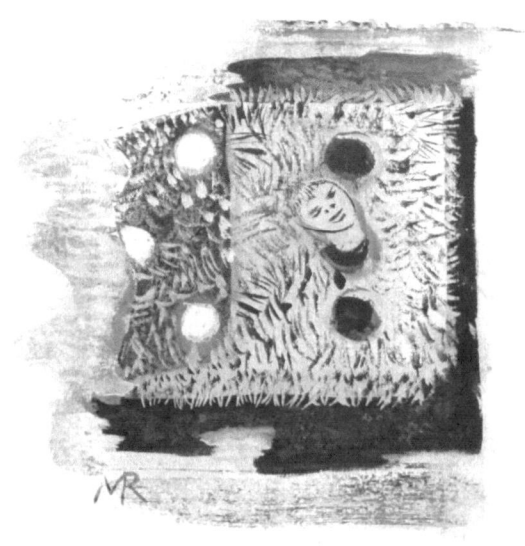

*"... Departure, arrival, freedom, survival –
It's all in the roll of the big furry dice... "*

A circle of friends
Philip Drew

De l'Obel was short and stout and breathless,
A mason, fond of his food and wine,
Devoted to all his small plump daughters.

Fuchs was a very snappy dresser. Pointed shoes
And elegant cravats were his passion.
He played the oboe rather well.

Zinn had bold unwinking eyes. His lady friends
All looked the same, clean, calm and solid,
With short fair hair and perfect teeth.

Buddle was never really clean-shaven.
He lived alone in the vicarage and collected stamps,
Grouping them by colour, like butterflies.

Dahl greatly enjoyed a party. When he told a story
His face glowed like fire. At the end
His laugh rattled the chandeliers. He was as robust

As Eschscholz was delicate, poor lad,
His mother tried in vain to make him rest.
At dances, his face glowed also, but too brightly.

Magnol always took the most comfortable chair. He loved
To be waited on by the young. "Relax," he would murmur,
Waving a scented handkerchief. "Be beautiful, my friends."

Forsyth stared at the wintry Northern stars.
The chill oppressed him and he dreamed of spring.
He arranged constellations along a twig.

(Dedicated to the Charlbury Garden Society.)

About Blue
Rob Stepney

Imagine someone stopped me in the street
And asked, ever so politely,
"Do you own a dog?"

Even if he were hard at my heels,
Obedient as leather on the leash,
I'd probably say "No".

Partly through pressure to be otherwise,
Not being with a dog is deep ingrained
In my identity.

But there are other times,
At the school gate,
Or on top of Brecon's Beacons –
After near three thousand feet of solid schlep –
When I see other dogs

And think they don't have half the heart,
Or pleasing symmetry of black and white,
Or lop-eared look of inquisition,
Or the sweet incongruity
One eye brown and one eye blue

Of our dog.

Homecoming
Eileen Dore

He gazes out of the window
Waiting for me to arrive.
I'm sure I'll see his eyes light up
As I walk along the drive.

It's lovely to have someone waiting,
Not to enter an empty place.
I open the door, and my heart is sure
As I look at his handsome face.
I say "Hello my dear one.
Have you missed me while I've been away?"
He doesn't reply, and I say with a sigh,
"I've had such an awful day.
The shops were all so crowded
And the prices all so high.
My back ached so bad
I thought I'd go mad
But, never mind dear, we'll get by.
I'll get you your favourite dinner
And together the evening we'll spend,
Sit by the fire
To our hearts' desire,
My faithful, feline friend."

Young Tolly
Elizabeth Llewellyn-Smith

On the duvet he reposes
All night long across my toeses
Lightly snores and gently dozes,
Tolly comfy as can be,
Which is not the case with me.
As he slumbers at his ease
I ask myself: "Has he got fleas?"

When I greet him in the morning
On the carpet he lies fawning,
Wriggling, stretching, grunting, yawning.
Then he gets a litle pat
And I say: "Good Morning, cat.
My, you *are* a super star.
What a handsome cat you are!"

The choir
Sheila Peacock

A gathering of people
Who dearly love to sing,
They don't do it for the money
But for the pleasure that it brings.

It releases them from daily toils,
The stresses of modern life.
Distances them from the argument
They had with husband or wife.

The harmonies they sing each week,
The struggle to reach top C,
Their voices singing for pure joy,
That sense of feeling free.

Different people, all walks of life,
But united just as one.
Pleasure etched on faces,
Singing is such fun!

Verses learned and memorised,
Harmonies galore.
Tenors, bass, sopranos,
Learning a new score.

Melodies are sung and worked upon,
The sounds are quite unique.
"Must we do it yet again?"
"Yes, we'll all be back next week!"

A gathering of people,
Friendships, warmth and love.
A feeling of a special bond,
Just one gigantic hug!

Suppertime blues
John Lanyon

(I guess I have a reputation for enjoying the finer things in life – fast cars, beautiful women, expensive clothes – but it's really my knowledge of fine wine that separates me from the rest of the crowd. So when a young lady was having a little difficulty at my local Co-operative Society supermarket, well, I just had to help …).

She said "I'm looking for a Red
That will work with fish"
I said "I'm a commis-chef
And you're my kind of dish!"

I'm as shy as a coconut
And, Baby, you knock me out
Come on over for supper
And I don't mean sauerkraut.

She said "Can you 'sauter'?"
I said "I'll jump for you the live-long day"
Sheesh! You've got me skewered
Like a holy man that's lost his way

I believe in cod,
Vinegar, chips and peas
I believe in kisses
That taste just like the seas.

I said "I'm a backwoodsman"
She said "I like your stile"
Come on in my kitchen,
I'm getting hungry, honey-chile.

I'll love you, baby
The way I love rock and roll
Till they lay me on that slab
And fillet my Jelly-Roll Sole

Help!
Margery Mayhew

Five a day, preferably organic
This advice makes me panic

Is this mince from a happy cow?
One thing is certain, it's not happy now

Are these eggs from free range hens?
All this worry makes me tense

Cash and time, these are needed
Then the advice can be heeded

But – exercise will do you good
Just try climbing Hixet Wood

Life is full of sin and stress
Why does it seem such a mess?

Oh pass me my book and the biscuit tin
It's cold outside, I'm staying in.

Keep Fit
Gareth Miller

Save contemplation for old age -
Keep active now.
Though meditation's all the rage
I've made a vow
To gaze upon my navel rather less,
For every time I do I find a mess.
By keeping fit and occupied, I guess
I'll find out how
To flee the cage
And take the narrow gauge,
Should fate allow.

The undressed chef
Nick Owen

Menu A: The gorilla

You have to grrrill a gorilla
Of this there can be little doubt
If you think you can boil
Then you're in for a toil
The gorilla will simply get out

Oh you have to grrrill a gorilla
Now why should this be, d'you suppose?
If you try to sauté
He will just walk away
And the pan will not reach to his toes

You have to grrrill a gorilla
There is no way that he's gonna fry
He has far too much hair
It just would not be fair
He just is not that sort of a guy

It's easy to grill a gorilla
He will lie there and think it's the sun
It will take him all day
And you won't have to stay
You just come back at night when he's done.

Hedgehog en croûte
Nick Owen

Do you want to cook a hedgehog?
Well, it's easy if you do.
I'm sad to say this recipe
Is really nothing new

First, tickle his tummy
Oh, yes, first tickle his tum.
If he does not die of laughing
You must whack him on the bum

Watch out for the prickles
As you cover him in clay
And if he's good and dead
I'm sure he will not get away

You place him in your oven
Just as if he were a pot
Don't touch him as you get him out
'Cause that would hurt a lot

When at last you crack him open
He will not begin to sing
But he does look rather scrumptious
Like a broken vase from Ming
And I simply have to tell you
He's a yummy, yummy thing.

Tiramisu

Bob Cockburn

Garibaldi was living on biscuits
And he didn't like what they had in Nice
He said, "Take me back to Napoli
There I could live quite happily
Just on tiramisu, and a second, third, fourth,
fifth, sixth, seventh, eighth, ninth piece."

Tiramisu is my religion
Tiramisu's what I believe
I'll eat mine and I'll eat yours too,
That's if you've got any to leave.

You can have your entrée into society
Your main course in your favourite eating haunts
But you can't beat a puddin'
Just as long as it's a good un
And I can't resist a piece of the pièce de résistance.

The heretics buy blancmange under the counter
In Hendon, Harrogate and Hell
And try to tempt me so succinctly
But fail to convince me:
Where's the joie de vivre in a crème caramel?

In Vienna I ate it hot
Everywhere else I ate it cold
I've had those tubs you buy from Sainsbury's
I've had it off, I've had it old

'Cos tiramisu is my religion
Tiramisu's what I believe
I'll eat mine and I'll eat yours too,
That's if you've got any to leave.

I've read the works of Aristotle,
Socrates and Plato too
But I find I can't accept
Any kind of raison d'être
That misses out the best
That ignores or just forgets
What reaches you faster than a jumbo jet
Hits as hard as a cigarette
Is so much sweeter than vinaigrette
Is more exciting than Wet Wet Wet
Is calling to you without a minaret
Will guide you through your life's upsets
It's the best created yet
It's the miracle of tiramisu.

The Lowry collection
Michael Moss

Men wear clogs, matchstick dogs
Smoking stacks (no girls in slacks)
Kids galore, and lots more
Bowler hats (no sign of spats)
Factory signs, railway lines
Busy folk (no bespoke)
Trousers spare, black, no flare
Shirt no collar, babies holler
Dirty snow, noses glow
Faces sallow, nowhere a sparrow
Tops and hoops, old man stoops
Striding lads, mums and dads
Tobacco pipes (no baby wipes)
Huge black boots. Siren hoots
To call the workers but no shirkers
Those up North know their worth
Industrial scene, wages mean
Humour there and despair
Nothing flowery,
It's art by Lowry

The portrait
Moira Wyatt

Under that mask, what do I see?
I poise the brush that strokes the board
With coloured paint.
A character, under all the show
Of bravado.
The tilt of eyebrow, slant of eye,
The quirky mouth, the cheeky grin,
Eyes give away the truth, of all the signs
I see in him.

A dab or two of blue to show
The pallor from the drugs he takes,
The red nose, bulbous, glows from wine,
Around the eyes are wrinkles fine,
A sadness blights the sitter's life,
Perhaps the loss of child or wife?
His grief can't hide in painted line,
Nothing escapes this brush of mine.

The straight lines of Giza
Mark Moss

Do we reveal ourselves as pedants to proclaim
Perfection in that pyramidal form rising
In graceful contrast to the golden desert sands?

Fifty-one point five degrees of elevation,
Perfection in alignment; testimonial,
Monumental proclamations of our power.

While we test heaven with towers, He forms desert
Perfection in dunes' undulating, sweeping flow,
In caressing curves of wind-kissed rippled ridges.

When time returns Giza to the sand, dust to dust
Perfection will bury memory of our folly
In sweeping strokes from a God who abhors straight lines.

DIY islands: Madeira

Peter Barber

Wait until things calm down
Then unreel your plumb-line.
Ensure your lava is truly
Vertiginous.
Be advised that you may find this
No piece of cake.
Let cool for a couple of aeons
Then thrust upward, parting fathoms.
Terrace all flows
With lush greens and a botany
That crams the tourist guides
With colours to go.

Then, and only then,
The graft all done,
Sit back, enjoy.

Skiathos

Elizabeth Llewellyn-Smith

Reincarnation? May be true.
If so I know what I should do:
If I'm allowed to choose my birth
For one more cycle on the earth,
A dolphin I should choose to be,
A dolphin of the Middle Sea.
For dolphins neither toil nor spin,
They have no sense of guilt or sin.
They are the swallows of the sea,
Dipping and skimming, light and free,
They leap and tumble as they please
Among the scattered Sporades.

Bad things were done in Ephesus
Rob Stepney

It wasn't like meeting the ghost of Pliny or St Paul,
Though both men when alive had walked these streets.
But it was an odd encounter, at the ruins' edge,
An old man with a bucket, on top of which were fig leaves.
They covered an embarrassment of snails.
To eat, he gestured.

I knew the word for "greens",
And mimed a gardener's displeasure at what snails ate.

We matched well in the matter of moustaches.
(His perhaps a little grizzlier.)
But his apparent taste for snails, and my distaste,
Seemed a natural limit to communication.
Then he undid a knotted handkerchief.
Inside, a ring with bearded head,
Delicately carved, in reverse relief.

This time he spoke: "I sell to eat. Good price for you."
From walks along the Evenlode, I knew the snails weren't Roman.
Nor, almost certainly, the ring.

Caveat emptor. For a wealth of reasons.

But what if it had been real, and I had bought it,
To save a man from eating snails, or out of avarice?
Worse things were done in Ephesus.

There was someone – it may even have been me –
Who dared disturb a brick, and with his own hand
Trace the maker's fingers as they formed the snakelike swirl
That keyed it to the mortar in antiquity.

The night of Alexander's birth, a madman torched the temple of Artemis,
Then the seventh wonder of the world.

Not only the dictator Syrpax, but all his family
Were stoned to death.
And bones found outside the walls of Ephesus
Show what it took to meet the appetite for bread and circuses.

One man fighting for his life, but others' entertainment
Was brought low, his knee smashed
By a weapon like a four-pronged knitting needle
Designed precisely for this purpose,
And a feature of the games in Ephesus.

Another's skull was neatly holed by two prongs of a trident.
A third had a problem with his back.
Not a slipped disc, you understand.
More a sword thrust from behind
That sheared two vertebrae
And then neatly sliced his heart.
The odds of dying in this trade's first season
Were two in three.

Caveat gladiator. For a range of reasons.

According to the city's famed philosopher, one Heraclitus,
Everything is flowing.
Perhaps because he'd seen much blood.
Bad things were done in Ephesus.

Follow my lieder

Mick Rooney

Up and down the U-Bahn
In and out the Stadt,
Lieder in the houses
Voices very flat.
Poor, appalled old Schumann
Turning in his grave.
Same for dear old Schubert,

A little peace he craves.
The family speaks of money
And pensions dwindling down.
The stock exchange a monster
Devouring all around.
Father's on his third wife,
Lives in steady style.
Still the Merc, a little yacht
But the future's looking so Kurt Weill.
Wants money from the children,
That they should pawn their lives,
Give back what he has given them
And what he gave his wives.
The singing from the basement,
The ripple of applause.
By clapping, are we purified.
And have they locked the doors?

It's grey the day, the leaves of fall
A baritone he drowns it all
His voice a hurricane of sound
His wife fat-legged but very proud
Their prize a daughter lean and svelte
The mother hugs, emotions felt.
Come the Sirens once again
Finds the audience poised for pain
Ambition's wailings, piano chords
Cracked notes, wrong notes, eardrums sore.
An ex-wife says she prays all day
For peace on earth, that her children may
Keep their father's outstretched palm at bay.
Some prosecco, corks a-popping
Some French-bread with cheesy topping
Some conversation hunting down the past
It's night. It's damp.
We're going home at last!
Goodnight Vienna!

Swagbelly

John Lanyon

Swagbelly drives a Robin Reliant
He never took no test and she's startin' to sway
Head down, white knuckles
He's suckin' sweets on the big highway

Don't knock me down, Mr Swagbelly
Don't knock me down

He don't worry about bumps and scratches
The clutch and the gearbox are leaking oil
Fags in the ashtray, foot on the floor
Cracks in the block and she's beginning to boil

Don't knock me down, Mr Swagbelly
Don't knock me down

No maps, no signs, no exits, no hassles
Fluorescent seat covers and a family of mice
Departure, arrival, freedom, survival –
It's all in the roll of the big furry dice

Don't knock me down, Mr Swagbelly
Don't knock me down

Farewell Fiesta

Tim Widdows

Annie had a little car
She loved it lots and lots
'Twas found just the other night
Burnt out and up on blocks

The car had special memories
Oh the trips that they have made

And sometimes reaching second gear
But only when she's brave

The trips you see were mainly short
A mile or two at most
The daily jaunts up to the farm
Is all the car could boast

But when it went on holiday
To Scotland – oh what a treat
A new lease of life was given
With Meg in the driver's seat

This car it wasn't flashy
Zooped up or full of bling
With no spare keys and dodgy brakes
Things were looking grim

But it had a bit of luxury
That was not of standard issue
In the form of her old army blanket
Which doubled as a tissue

Now to those people who did steal it
We hope you had just cause
Cause when she finds out who you are
She'll knee you in the balls!

Night life

Dorothy Day

As bright moon slips behind a cloud
The shadows deepen in the wood
Badgers forage on the leafy floor
Wily old fox slips from his lair
The bats their frantic dance begin
Dipping, weaving on the wing

Darkness hides the crouching cat
Waiting to pounce on mice who squat
Beneath a headstone upright stood
Like a sentry guarding the dead
But the night is silently alive
With ghostly hunters on the move
Searching for their hapless prey
This game of hide and seek they play
Until the night's cloak is torn
And cast away by the breaking dawn.

The countryside
Dorothy Day

The cock's loud crow rends the air
In acknowledgement of the new day
Joining him in tribute to the dawn
The choir of birds voice their song
The thick shroud of morning mist
Reveals, as it slowly lifts,
The sun's rays cresting the hill.

Gradually warming the early chill
Cows restlessly milling by the gate
Milking time, and they think they're late.
Timid rabbits emerge from burrows
Gulls calling loudly follow the furrows
Made by the big red tractor ploughing
The field ready for seed corn sowing.

Milkman whistles as he drives his float
Bottles clinking merrily in the back
Even the postie has a spring in his step
Hoping the promise will be kept
By the coming day as it unfolds
To show itself and all it holds.

V
Past times

*"…She combed your hair so blond, so fine…
the memory as clear as summer wine…"*

Shards of now

Mark Moss

Time etches eternity in glass.
I cast backward glances like
Blows against the pane

To shatter reflections,
Find clarity in cuts from shards
Of the cubist past

Where devil's food cake is still chocolate,
Where cars cast to carpet
Paint Monet over madness

Where a child's voice
Is a night song whispered
Across the infinite distance between us now.

"Daddy, I had a scary dream. Daddy!"

Hindsight is tunnel vision
For the truth, digital focus
For things too close for clarity

Where the ghost-touch of a small hand
Still lingers in mine,
Etched in glass…etched in glass.

But the glass is a mirror,
Not a window.
Unbreakable

It breaks me
Showering me with shards of now
That cut all the way to the heart.

Winter bath

Hilda Reed

The memory is clear as summer wine:
she stroked the swansdown of your golden back
and let her fingers ripple down your spine.

The youngest, in the bath before the grime
of older children, cleaned and scrubbed and wrapped
in memory as clear as summer wine.

Then warm and dry and sitting for a time
around the fire that flared with dusty slack,
she let her fingers ripple down your spine.

Absorbed, she combed your hair so blond, so fine,
searched your head, untangled stubborn tats;
the memory as clear as summer wine.

She brushed it gently, bringing out the shine,
ignored the protests of your flailing hands
and let her fingers ripple down your spine.

Though now your backbone carves a harder line,
the down no longer softening its track,
in memory as clear as summer wine
her fingers still can ripple down your spine.

You nudged my muse
Eithne Dillon

You nudged my muse
And opened up my silken box of memories.
So many golden memories, precious and sweet,
Whose recollection still brings a tingle to my backbone.
Others sad, poignant, full of regret,
Marking the loss of loved ones and sadder times.
But most of all, I recall those special days
That can never be forgotten,
Brought back in an instant by a scent on the wind,
Shaft of sunlight on water, snowdrops and bluebells
In woods where we wandered in the spring
Marvelling at newness of life and all things new –
New love, new life, new home.
But always that lingering remembrance of times past
When life was opening up before us
And love was spread upon us
Like a mantle, protecting tender plants
From the first frosts of life.

II

My muse led me back across the years,
Remembering days well spent on hill
With brothers, friends and dog.
The Nut Wood often drew us to explore
A place only we seemed to know,
A single piece of woodland on our hill
And we would wander there until
The next adventure drew us on.
And then at last the day was done
And we would wander home again
Bare legs frayed by bracken and heather,
Homeward bound, soaked and muddy,
Glowing with the rain and wind upon our faces,
Hair all a-tangle;
Then into hot bath with sponge and soap

Once more made clean
And wrapped in rough towel
Before our mother's roaring fire.

There at the fire we'd toast our bread
And eat it warm with hot sweet tea,
Toast, overloaded with butter and homemade jam,
And we were cosily wrapped up in family
While dark night stayed outside our home
And rain battered the world outside.

Now when we meet, my brothers and I,
We remember these things of childhood with affection.
As the old tales get better year by year
And children and grandchildren now ask
'Tell us the story about …'
They want to know the old tales,
The ones that make us laugh and sigh,
Of things we find so amusing, and the 'why'.
As each new generation grows,
So their memories too will grow,
The heritage of our family conspiring together,
Making history for them as they remember
All we brought to them in life and love and laughter.

We who remain
Robert Macefield

The flowers of spring
Hilltops full with morning dew
Remembered songs
Dancing in groves
Of oak and yew
Precious, most sacred
Avalon
All these years long gone
We who travel through time
Following streams of love that flow
A Royal Court built
With the powers of Myrridin's rhyme
Mirrors to contain
A grail cup to find
Many paths we follow
Sent that day to this
From Ceridwen's hollow
Camelot we miss
So many knights
Have fallen, lost their way
Half remembered paths to steer
This world in which we stay
Few left who dream
Here with us now
Alongside us still
Unseen
The Table Round
Our spiral wheel
Enemies we confound
Ancient grail they cannot steal
Hold in your heart
This noble band
For we travel still
Through ancestral lands
And if you know those
Who would blame

In anger, fear or controlling shame
Send us your prayers
We hear them clear
Dispelling the fog
Of many a year
So I sit before the Sacred Well
Knowing this rhyme my last farewell
Losing reason, mind
Ties that bind
The grail I someday hope
To find
Returning through hollowed hills
To where I know, can feel
Is the centre
My Medicine Wheel

So wish us well
No sad refrain
The Knights of Old

Some still remain

A dream of our youth

Peter John Colyer

Heads together, side by side, walking.
"What's the matter?" you said to my frown.
I looked straight at you. Eyes together.
"You are," I said, meaning "I love you."
And "Where is this leading us?"
You understood.
"Don't worry," you said.
"It will be all right. We'll find the way."

It was. We did.
We will.

Then
Brigid Allen

Strawberries, warm from the plant,
Were as kindly as religion.

Crimson peony buds peeled
In a child's exploratory fingers.

Stripes were significant.
(See the red-and-white railway signals;
The thrusting pole at the barber's;
Schoolboys' quarter-coloured caps.)

The floor was near,
Dark, a threat,
Like a blow on the head or the grave.
But the sun, swaying downwards
Like a tin-lid through water,
Glowed between four compressed fingers
With the radiant scarlet of blood.

Memories of Witney
Eileen Dore

I remember walking to St Mary's School
A gas mask on my arm.
I remember spending all day at the Bathing House
Never coming to harm.
I remember sitting on the wall of Marriotts Close
Asking Yanks "Any gum, chum?"
I remember Sunday walks along Duck Lane
With Dad and Mum.
I remember "minnowing" down the Hills and Mountains
And crayfishing too
On the banks of the Windrush, all summer through.
I remember with horror the nit-nurse at school
Searching our heads for lice.

I remember the teachers, Miss Barnes, "Percy" Wiggins,
And – oh yes – Mrs Pratley. She was nice.
I remember hopscotch, rag and skipping
In the cold school yard.
Drinking our milk at lunchtime,
With chunks of bread and lard.
I remember evacuees from London
Seeking a little peace
From the bombing of their city
Which never seemed to cease.
I remember the night two bombs hit our town.
St Mary's school was damaged,
But they couldn't knock it down.
I remember the celebrations when the war was finally won,
Dancing in the Market Square, parties in the streets.
Us kids had never known such fun.
I remember taking rabbit skins to Houghton's yard,
Getting thruppence for every one.
And collecting rose hips for the chemist,
They seemed to weigh a ton!
I remember the joy when Witney Feast returned,
Couldn't wait to get to the Leys
To spend the money I'd earned.
I remember so many things about the years gone by.
And should you smile and reminisce
Thee must be as old as I.

Thoughts

Eileen Dore

I walked along the lonely shore
My footsteps to be seen.
Waves came in and washed them away,
As if I'd never been.
Deep in thought, I gazed
At that great expanse of sea
And hoped that in its vast green depths
It retained a memory
Of me.

Summer '95

Eileen Dore

Summer sounds are music to my ears,
Hullabaloo of Wimbledon
"Oohs, Ahhs" and cheers.
The splashing of children in water
Takes me down "memory lane".
Summer lasted forever,
Never a spot of rain.
But now as I relax in our garden
Nothing can surpass
The sound of my husband's footsteps
And the tinkle of ice in a glass.

Cobwebs

Gareth Miller

Here in the unlit attic of my mind
I stumble round to see what's left behind,
Tripping on junk I've stored across the years -
Unsorted thoughts and themes, unfocused fears,
A failed romance, a ruse, a thwarted plan,
Cobwebbed in every dark recess I scan.
All these and other fantasies I find
Within the unlit attic of my mind.

Have I the will to renovate this loft?
Yes, but you must be ruthless now, not soft
Or sentimental – chuck it all away.
Go light the bonfire now without delay.
No more recycled dreams, no fancy schemes,
No second-hand ideas, no fresh regimes.
Open a window, hoover up the dust,
Buy furniture that's new and readjust.

Christmas spirit
Moira Wyatt

Christopher, the eldest son,
said "We're going skiing, having fun.
Cavorting in the winter sun.
We won't be with you, Mother dear.
Perhaps we'll come another year..."

Said Katie, "Sorry mum, my boyfriend's
parents want their son, and asked for me,
as well, to come.
I'm sure I need to be quite bold.
You won't want us, as you're so old."

And James spoke up, and told her that,
as he'd got an awful cold,
He thought his mother should be told.
Old people mustn't catch the bug.
He'd stay at home, wrapped in a rug.

As mummy dear put down the phone
she realised she'd be alone.
It proved to her, her inmost fears -
she tried to stem the floods of tears.

Until a thought came in her head
She'd fly to "gay Paree" instead.

Christopher soon broke his leg,
and James recovered from the flu,
A lovers' tiff ditched Katie too.
And though they all tried hard to beg
for Christmas cheer, with mother dear.
The phone was silent. Where was she?
Why! Having fun in gay Paree!

Echoes of summer in Pezenas
Moira Wyatt

Echoes of children's voices
On the marble stairs.
Echoes of screams and happy laughter
Children with no cares.
The pool lies silent, blank and cold.
The trees stir not to climbing feet.
The house rests quiet, peaceful, old.
No one to swing the garden seat.

Bring back the sun, the summer heat.
Bring back the family, all the noise.
The cherries ripe enough to eat,
For plundering by hungry boys.
Small girl dancing, racing feet,
And squabbling over favourite toys.
The ping pong table's steady beat.
Oh, for the creaking of the garden seat.

Cricket at Worcester
Mike Dix

The sun is shining and the train is on time
We travel expectantly up the line
The stations are small and the travellers few
But an hour later the cathedral's in view
After the green fields in summery state
We're into the town, walking fast, can't be late
Past bakers and books and clothing on hooks
Past cafés and banks, but not today thanks.
Over the river where the swans always gather
We pause to admire them, it isn't much farther.

The turnstiles click as we pay for a ticket
What a wonderful sight, the sun on the wicket.

Seats are found and we look round the ground
Time for a drink, the coffee cups clink
The toss is taken and the umpires stride out
A splendid sight, of this we've no doubt.
The game is the focus for the next seven hours
But there are many other topics to test mental powers.

A bacon bap brunch and a pint before lunch
The picnic is fine with a bottle of wine
But teatime's pleasure is tea and cakes
Those excellent tea ladies certainly know how to bake.
The hours slip by in a world of our own
Soon have to make our way happily home
Leaving the scene, the cathedral watching over it
A day out to remember in dark cold December.

(This poem was first read in public on the morning train to Worcester, 9th September 2004, by the then President of Charlbury Cricket Club, the late Mike Dix. Contributed by Maureen Walker.)

Damp wait

Mike Dix

We're waiting for the rain to stop. Plip plop
We're waiting for the rain to stop
'Camping' in our wooden hut
With summer smells of sweat and grass
Linseed oil and swelling damp
One needs his pipe, let him pass
He'll check the prospects while he's out

We're waiting for the rain to stop
Has anyone here seen the mop?
Friends and family, girlfriends and dogs
Let's hope that someone's cleaned the bogs.
It's coming through the ceiling now
Not through the cellar and out the door

Like it did that time before!
Bricks and mortar are what we need
Not leaking timber and wet grass seed

We're waiting for the rain to stop
'Camping' in our wooden hut; door shut
Waiting for the sun to shine
Waiting for tea time
We haven't got a set of covers
This game will be just 20 overs
When will it stop? Plip, plop.

(Contributed by Maureen Walker.)

The school walk

Moira Wyatt

I saw lots of dogs on my way to school,
Lazy dogs, silly dogs, playing the fool.
Young dogs, old dogs, having dog games.
Wuffing and barking and growling rude names.
Tan dogs, black dogs, spotted and white -
What will I do if they all start a fight?

I saw a girl and boy strolling along,
He was singing her a sweet wee song.
I asked my Mummy for a little boy too,
To sing me a song about being true.
But she only smiled and said "Perhaps one day."
Now wasn't that a funny thing for her to say?

I saw an artist with a long red beard,
He was wearing clothes that were awfully weird.
What will he do with his beard at night?
Put it in rags and curl it up tight?
Or plait it in pigtails, like I do mine?
If you find out, will you tell me sometime?

I saw a little bird on a bare tree,
He sang a little song that was just for me.
He cheered up the streets with his chirpy song,
And I felt happier running along.
So I sang to my teacher 'cos she looked sad,
But she put me in a corner and said that I was bad!

Cissie Gomm

Ethel Thornett

The girls were playing rounders
And all was blithe and gay
When suddenly a piercing shriek
Bedimmed the light of day.
"Oh! Who is hurt?" I asked in dread
With terror well nigh dumb.
"Oh that!" they said. "That's nothing.
It's only Cissie Gomm."

(As recited by Mrs R H Young to her niece, April 2006. Ethel Thornett was a senior teacher at Charlbury School. Cissie Gomm, who lived on Crawborough, was known as a child for her piercing shrieks.)

VI
A rich miscellany

*"What she wants requires me
To bathe naked
In front of her hunting dogs"*

Is there a book inside you?
Adrian Lancini

They say everybody has a book inside them
so I went to my local hospital for an X-ray
to see if it was true.
It wasn't.

I had a heart, lungs and kidneys
but no book.

My hopes had been temporarily raised
when the radiologist found my appendix.
But it wasn't that kind of appendix.

I was disappointed.

Sebastian Faulks, Doris Lessing, Nick Hornby
all had books inside them.
Why haven't I?

But then I thought
maybe there's someone out there
with a book inside them, about me!

Maybe it's in them right now.

Maybe it's just waiting to come out.

Maybe it's inside you?

An ABC of poetry
Rob Stepney

A is for April, "the cruellest month", before
Bs are properly buzzing.
C is in Charlbury, though we're miles from the shore.
D's for decay, which we hope's long in coming.

E for emotion.
F could be effing, and blinding too. But perhaps
G is for genial, and
H for honest – not that
I am the subject.

J for joyful wagging of a
K nine tail.
L for Elliott.
M for metre.
N for end, which is
Omega too.
P is a problem if you're stuck in a
Q.

R for rhyme.
S for essence.
T for two and
U for me.
V for Victory, and if I
Double you, that would be
X for unknown. But surely
Y is for wine leading to
Zed zed zed for bed.

Words

Eithne Dillon

Rhymes are words to memorise,
Words that take you by surprise.
Gleaming, golden, starlit light,
Words of day and words of night.
Black as coal with swordlike edge
Driving in a hateful wedge.
Swarming bee and cackling hen
Bring us down to earth again.
Words that whine and words that whimper,
Laughing smile or silly simper.
Words expressed in platitudes
Some described with 'attitude'.
Other words that are so charming
Words like 'dearest', 'sweetheart', 'darling'.
Words can catch you unawares,
Can attract some doubtful stares.
Unkind words to brother, sister,
Open wound or oozing blister.
Words that warm, like soup and toast,
They're the ones I love the most.
Words of comfort, words of caring
They're the ones I should be sharing.
Safe like blanket, warm and cosy
Scented flowers tied in a posy.
Give me words that warm the heart
And from them never, never part.

Mercy
Anthony Landale

Athena, Goddess of thinking,
Is always armoured and always right.
That is why I fear her.
Of all in the pantheon she
Has least to do with mercy.
She ridicules the plaintiff
And defeats every prayer.
But what she wants, ahh,
What she wants requires me
To bathe naked
In front of her hunting dogs.

Dreamwalker
Robert Macefield

Wind over a dusty trail
Dreaming lizard blinks
Clinging
I see the fire in her eyes
Letting go
The smoke from a pipe
Burning
Ashes in the mind
I die
I fly
A child of Persephone I
Never-ending
Who to mourn passing
Footprints in Eternity
Loss
Emptying
Nothing left
Sorry
Wind over a dusty trail

Dreaming lizard…
Blinks

Transience
Jane Corbett

The first blush of blue across the wood
The new leaves pushing up through the dead
Bright green moss on a rotting branch
Wild honey bee sniffing out the nectar
The cuckoo catching a bell in its call

And there is only this
Watching my breath rise and fall

The moment in the woods at dawn
The night birds yielding to the light

The warmth of the spring sun on my cheek

Always whispering
Anthony Landale

The soul, I understand, does not care for success or failure.
It hungers only for the gristle of experience.
But why should this be?
It is because it is only then that we awaken
To the ecstatic moment.
Only then that we dare that edge
Only then that we finally surrender.
And that is why the soul never stops whispering
To me to fly.
And why I have a thousand reasons to deny it.

Jam and Jerusalem
Tim Widdows

The Women's Institute, well what can we say?
Little old ladies chattering away.
That was the image we all used to know,
How times have changed, and they've gone with the flow.

Once a month at the hall they all would meet,
Along with the guest who had been booked to speak.
Everyone hoping it won't be a bore,
As it doesn't take much for Angie to snore.

All the committee sit front of the hall,
With President Jones presiding it all.
The table looks lovely, the flowers look posh,
And thanks to our June there's plenty of nosh.

And if it's your birthday you're in for a treat,
You're handed a posy that's pretty but cheap.
A different person is given this chore,
It's amazing what's made with sweepings from the floor.

Just like the seasons – coffee mornings there's four,
They trundle to Charlbury with cakes galore.
Teabread and scones – Victorias too,
And Meg's plum jam which doubles as glue.

Yes, at the Corner House they peddle their wares,
A knitted tea cosy and Graeme's old flares.
An Elvis recording that jumps on each track,
The Maeve Binchy novel the library wants back.

Lots of fundraising to fill up the books,
The Farmhouse Big Breakfast with Carol the cook.
But now she's retired – the looks start to fade,
A blue rinse now beckons to join this brigade.

So on to the darts team which really works hard
To search for a pub from which they're not barred.
The game when it's over they all give a cheer,
It's time to get down to some serious beer.

Joan Madeley, Ann Timbs – the list it goes on,
Please do forgive me if I missed anyone.
The WI – it's amassed quite a troupe,
Of elderly women with boobs on the droop.

Yes all you ladies in the WI,
You can all walk the streets with your heads held up high.
Everyone knows you are doing your best,
It's all jam and Jerusalem – in your knitted string vest!

(Written at the request of Tim's mother, for the Spelsbury WI.)

Braggadocio
John Lanyon

I've got seven suits
In seven shades of grey
I've got people who tell me
Just what I want to say
I've got more froth
I've got more spin
Than the cappuccino
I like dipping in
They all say "Hey, Joe…
I dig your braggadocio."

Braggadocio …
That's the mojo
That lets you in the dojo
Braggadocio…
Hear me on a talk show
A cup of tea?

Does that fit my beverage portfolio?
Braggadocio ...
I'll get back to you on that one.
Braggadocio ...
Just remind me what I really feel
Just remind me what I really feel

World like mine
Peter Head

I shut down my body
And nobody knows
Forget it all
The feeling goes
Shut down my head
The feelings stop flowing
I've lost the path
And forgotten where I'm going
Deep in my mind
Nobody knows
Forget the feeling
It comes and goes
Shut down my brain
Your feelings you're showing
Turn it back on
Bad feelings are growing
I've turned off my heart
Where nobody goes
Shut down my system
She comes, she knows
Don't worry about me
I'm doing just fine
That feeling goes
In the sniff of a line
Don't worry about me
I'm doing just fine
But I'd never let you
Into a world like mine

The case for late October
Mick Rooney

Moon fit to burst
Late October, organ-lofted sky,
A threnody of distant constellations.
Beneath
The muzzled architectural clutter,
Local tribes are gathered in.
Television moons are realer still
(illuminating stars
of sudless soaps)
From her den the urban fox
Pads soft with purpose
Through wasteland sprawl
To river bank, avoiding traffic
To hunt up water rat or vole
Or dine on fish and chips
And pizza scraps.
Unsated, she-fox points her head.
Screaming, she divides the stars
In this autumnal docu-soap.
The verdict comes
Unproven. Case dismissed!
And off she goes.

October Evensong
Gareth Miller

Crisp crimson leaves adorn the garden floor;
Warm light of evening's autumn sun streams through the window
    pane;
And momentary, sensory, the Nunc Dimittis spells
The ripened prophet's poignant last refrain.

Wireless, the chant suspended in mid-air;
Preces provoke responses, psalms wring sacramental tears;

And polyphonic melodies of Tallis and of Byrd
Serve to subdue my elemental fears.

Windless, the leaves lie dormant, undisturbed;
Prayers are collected, intercessions flood the silent room;
Skies from the west turn grey from blue and chill the October air,
And broadcast anthems gather up the gloom.

Dear Nine-to-Five Existence

Dear Nine-to-Five Existence,

I hereby give four weeks notice for terminating my contract with you.

My reasons for leaving are numerous but my mind was finally made up on a magical cliff top in Cornwall. In an inebriated state, with the sun about to rise over the ocean, I came across a most sobering sight – an astoundingly vivid red flower.

I finally woke up to the beauty around me. How can I possibly spend half my life trapped between four walls when all this is going on outside?

It's absurd.

I laughed at the absurdity of it. I laughed loudly and vowed there and then to leave you as soon as possible.

So I'm leaving you.

I wish you all the best for the future.

Yours sincerely,

Adrian Lancini

Sisters

Hilda Reed

My sister is a monster.

Crashing the plates and clattering knives
she's laying the table. Beware! For your lives
are endangered: she's not at her best in the morning.

Slamming the door and scattering post
she's on her way out, and she's making the most
of her exit. Thank god she's gone out for the morning.

Returning at lunchtime, and looking quite bright,
she soon finds the meal isn't turning out right
and she grumbles. She's no better now than this morning.

The afternoon drags as she knits and she sews;
she curses the stitches that snag as she goes
to cast off. But she'll sort it all out – in the morning.

Switching the channels she hogs the remote,
she's missing EastEnders, she's getting provoked
into violence. She'll do just the same in the morning.

Later that night, disturbed from her sleep
she storms round the house and makes sure that she keeps
us from sleeping. She's sure to be worse in the morning.

My sister *is* a monster.

Vic's sticks
Eithne Dillon

1 The sticks speak

We are brothers, cut from the same chestnut tree,
Fashioned into fine straight sticks
We endure the steam and sweat
Until our hard core melts
And we are soft and pliable,
Bent upon ourselves in one long loop,
Tied with twine to secure the curve,
Then trimmed to fit
Hands that will hold us fast for years.

And so it was that Vic found us;
Held us, tried us out,
And we fitted him so well.
"Just the job!", he said,
And took us home to Charlbury.

2 Vic speaks

The sticks? –
Ah, they've been with me these last forty years.
Bought them in Chippy –
They're chestnut, you know.
Don't know why, but most sticks are chestnut.
Now this one, the left one, you look and see;
See those marks down there – they're feet and inches
Two foot – comes in handy
When you need to measure something.
And there, see that notch on the top?
That just rubbed like that when it was resting against the lathe!
Now, the right one, that's a bit shorter than the left,
Broke it when trying to shift a wardrobe,
And there's a little notch down there –
Caught in the saw one day, just a nick.

No, you can't mistake one for the other,
You hold it and see –
Ah, those grooves are my fingers and thumb
Wearing away the wood.
No, you wouldn't think it was possible
That wood would wear like that.
Forty year ago, bought them in Chippy.

3 The sticks' final speech

Life was so full for forty years.
From shop to home and up the street and back.
What conversations we enjoyed!
What people we met!
Then in the evening
We'd soon be down the garden
In our own world.
Oh, life was never boring!
We had so many uses –
Things to pick up, branches to pull down,
Oven doors to open and close –
We were always on duty
Ready to serve,
And all the while the old clocks ticked.

And as he began to leave us
We were set aside, put out of the way
As other hands helped,
Fetched and carried,
Until our usefulness was gone.
Perhaps it was then that we retired.
But he left his mark upon us
And anyone who picks us up
And holds us
Will feel the handholds
Of his hands forever.

This poem springs from one of many conversations with my friend and neighbour, Vic Brackenbury, who died 07/07/07. It is dedicated to his memory.

Sculpture of life

Peter Head

He who made you so beautiful
Put on the earth with the purpose to fulfil
Glad I wasn't the master sculptor
Wish I knew how he made her
Carved her face from a rock
The mystery of life his key can unlock
With God the greatest artist on earth
Tried to buy the world, he asked its worth
What's on offer – diamonds and gold?
I'm sorry my son, the world's been sold
This is not a universe made for man
You're all part of a bigger plan
As for life it does go on
I've found another earth and another sun
And as for heaven, the doors are closed
Till such time as the world gets the love it shows
Sell me your secrets, sell me your plan
Give me the earth, I'll control man
On that land, blood man pours
You've ruined my world, you can have it, it's yours
In the corner of a universe a glimmer of hope
Looking through the eye of my telescope
Something green, something's growing
A star's burned out and started glowing
Mountains tall, seas and land
With God in the middle a rock in his hand

Seed
Robert Macefield

A seed flying in the breeze
Over rocks
Fields
Trees

Twisting through lakes
In the twilight
Stars swimming in the reflection
Of the seas

Over mountains rich with history
I bud and bloom and belong
A chorus of many colours
More and all of these... my song

Birds pass me on in jest, as a lark
Rolling into forests dense and dark
A seed am I, travelling on to creation
A notion to conceive

Simple and small, unnoticed
Alive with all potential
Nature's blueprint essential
I do not have to believe

Paths twisting, turning and wending
Nature's wishes concealed in a blending
No duty other than me, just be
As my heart buds forth and heals

This myth is woven... with a wish
That someday this pod in human form
Travelling the dream through a violent storm

Will be woken...
With a kiss.

Mystery
Robert Macefield

Power lines
Between light and dark
Twilight dancers of the dawn
Glowing so very fine
Crossing nights' starry mornings
Warriors breaking illusion's rhythms
Mirror images without reflections
Linking the stars so very few
Sacred clowns holding true
Stretching the highwire
Bridges of the abyss
Travellers with icecold fire
Balancing the cosmic scales
Outward play
Inner battleground
Jugglers of fortune
Death's doorway full
With sacrifice
To life
Gravity without pull
Tightrope walkers of the abstract
Spirit they entice
Faultline doctors
Skimming the waves
Rainbow hunters
Volcanic obsidian, colours of black
Nature's message held intact
Hobos of perfect rhyme
Pioneers of chance
Clocks out of time
Consorts in advance
Certainty a must
Upon this cable
Of dust
Refined artists, masters of
Trust

Power lines
Between light and dark
Somersault runners of awareness
Anchors of the air so few
Pure stress
Want to be free?
Arrows of forever
Do you wish to be..?

Head bus driver

Anon

She's the latest 'show' breed of headteacher
Designer suits are a regular feature
Superb at public speaking
Totally charming
Apparently at ease
At first, nothing alarming.

Enslaved to accountability
Obsessed by uncluttered surfaces
Turned on by targets, determined to increase A*-C passes
by fair means or foul.
Truly a Blairite Babe, dedicated to data
It wasn't too long before we began to hate her.

She's on a global mission
'To promote teaching and learning.
No expulsions either please!'
All the naughties leave by 'managed moves' – as do the staff.

Dissent is not allowed
Open dialogue is ploughed
Staff meetings became lectures --
I call it wrap-around fascism.

And we noticed how
trusted, long-serving, experienced staff resigned

with no job to go to.
Others went overnight on long-term sick leave.
Senior Management doubled --
Interviews fudged and rerun
'To appoint quality'

Support staff were feted, then dumped.
Scandals of gross misconduct by some staff were swept under her
    special purchase carpet
Disciplinary letters for minor matters were handed out like sweets.
Staff were listed: 'Blockers' or 'Enablers'
Thousands were spent on weekend residentials
so her 'Enablers' could learn dodgy American business management
    strategies
which contaminate the soul.
We noticed.

'Blockers' were removed by underhand manoeuvres, all various,
    double-dealing at every corner.
Staff had one version of events, senior management another,
Governors another and parents another.
Clever fragmentations.

She did not honour promises
and told outrageous liesies.
All school meetings were planted with her spiesies.
The charm offensive that she does so well
could not seduce Tory borough personnel
who she openly despises.

Our dastardly Head with arctic eyes
is a full-blown narcissist in disguise.
Her door is always firmly shut,
time for our school continually cut.
"She's out", "She's busy", "Not today",
explains a well-rehearsed PA.

Our Head pushed twelve staff off her 'bus'
and then it stalled.
The unions were flexing their muscles,

Formal grievances landed on her desk.
Obstacles were appearing on her career cruise highway.

For two weeks we saw nothing of the Head.
Had she taken her 'bus' for repairs?
She returned with a new job instead
Soon she'll be leaving and nobody cares.

When might time have stopped?
Rob Stepney

After radio but before TV
Post "the pill" but pre HIV

Let's have the fax but not the mobile phone
Last orders, but not the long walk home

Before Altamont, but after Woodstock
Post Dr Who but pre Dr Spock

When grass was greener, before hydroponic skunk
Pre New Romantics but post Sid Vicious Punk

Before Modern Art—and Never Mind the Pollocks

Après garlic but avant nouvelle cuisine
Between then, and the might have been

When a cheese is poised between ripeness and rot
Just before your spoon enters the honey pot

In the crisp hours before slush follows snow
When you know you must part but before you must go

Between an inspiration and its edits
The climax and the credits

Or between the credit and the crunch

Between the future and the past
The first breath and the last

Between the rush of revolution
And the onset of reality

Post World War II but pre World War III

Nocturne

Gareth Miller

At 4am I lie awake
And contemplate each thought opaque,
And try to make coherent themes
Out of the refuse of my dreams,
And churn each old familiar line,
And seek to find some grand design.
In vain I scan my mental space
In search of some redeeming grace.

At 6 o'clock I acquiesce- -
No meaning found, I rise and dress,
And navigate my daily round,
Where trivial tasks and chores abound.
In such as these fulfilment lies.
There is no greater goal or prize.
In modest duties, humbly done,
An everlasting crown is won.